About th

Julian Hutchings lives in ]
    the author of twelve other works,
    prolific YouTuber, a passionate road cyclist and a
    proud member of Old Portlians Cycling Club.

# Old Friends
# To
# The End

## Cycling from Land's End to
## John O'Groats

# Julian Hutchings

Rock the Ground Productions

Also by Julian Hutchings

Cycling Shorts and Cycle Clips
Tour de Fiction
Rachel and the Talking Fish
Tell Me that it Doesn't Rhyme
The Eyes Have it, The Eyes Have it
The Secret Diary of an Indoor Cat
Dentures, Guns and Money:
The Diary of a Home Care Worker
Unreliable Death
Shylah and the Nesting Dolls
The Monument
The Marmot Murders
Love's Lost in Girona

## Thanks

Bike Adventures: www.bikeadventures.co.uk
Ride Leaders: Richard, Martin, Mike
All the riders in the group
Jon for the lift to Penzance
Simon for nutrition advice
Robert for IT advice
Clare for teaching me about page breaks and being
a life-long friend

Special thanks to Ian – my ride partner: here's to
the next one, matey!

And always: Jane, Rachel and Joel

*It's like our visit to the moon*
*Or to that other star*
*I guess you go for nothing*
*if you really want to go that far*

*Death of a Ladies Man, Leonard Cohen*

# Before

I started cycling seriously in 2011 and as the years passed, became more and more passionate about it – some would say obsessive. I had undertaken numerous trips abroad and had ridden in Girona[1], Majorca, Lanzarote, Tenerife and Sardinia as well as in the Alps, the Pyrenees and the Dolomites; I'd climbed Ventoux four times as well as Alpe d'Huez and completed many European sportives including 4 times the Tour of Flanders, twice Liege Bastogne Liege[2] and Paris Roubaix and Amstel Gold once each.

But Land's End to John O'Groats had never been high on my bucket list – in fact it didn't even appear on my bucket list, not that I had one. I knew many people who had done it and all their tales seemed to revolve around endless rain and a ride that seemed closer to misery than enjoyment, and I preferred Europe and the lure of Continental cycling. A group of riders from my club – the Old Portlians – had ridden it in 2007 and it had rained every day, conditions were brutal and one of the riders – Les Roberts[3] who was riding in aid of Parkinson's research – had been blown off his bike in high winds on Shap Fell. It didn't seem like fun.

And then Covid happened.

---

[1] Love's Lost in Girona, Amazon 2020

[2] The Monument, Amazon 2019

[3] From Wits' End to John O'Groats by Les Roberts: Authorhouse 2009

I had met Ian in 2018 on a Marmot Tours[4] trip to the Dolomites and we discovered a shared interest in cycling for enjoyment as well as the challenge. We toiled up the Passo Stelvio, stopping regularly to enjoy the view; and we toiled up the Gavia, scene of Andy Hampsten emerging from a blizzard in the 1988 Giro; and we toiled up the Mortirolo, stopping regularly because we needed to; and we toiled up the Giau and the Pordoi and the Campolongo – but we beat them all.

We met up again the following year on a trip to the Picos in North-western Spain, again with Marmot Tours and this time toiled up the Lagos de Covadonga, and many other climbs although Ian made it up the Angliru while I packed and climbed into the support van. I wrote a murder mystery novella about the trip and published it on Amazon[5].

We arranged to meet again in 2020 on a trip visiting the Classic Cols of the Southern Alps - Bonette, Turini, Madone - but that had to be deferred for a year due to Covid. However, as March 2021 loomed and travel restrictions were still in place, it seemed unlikely that our July trip would happen.

'Fancy doing something else?' I said to Ian, one day over the phone. 'In this country?'

'LeJog,' he said, 'I did it in 2007 for charity, took 14 days. I want to do it again, but quicker.'

---

[4] Marmot Tours: www.marmot-tours.co.uk
[5] The Marmot Murders, Amazon 2019

'Um,' I said, 'let me think about it. Let's do some research.'

He texted me the next day.

'I've booked,' he said, and gave the name of the company – Bike Adventures[6].

So I booked, about £1400 plus single room supplement as there was no way I was sharing a room with Ian or anyone else, and he felt the same, and so the die was cast. It was to be 9 days, an average of 100 miles per day, with no rest days. It sounded tough.

I was (am) an experienced and reasonably strong club cyclist, regularly riding 5 to 7000 miles a year and had done several multi-day journeys previously, so I wasn't overly concerned about being able to manage LeJog – as I had started to call it. Nonetheless, I mapped out a training plan – in the 4 months before our jaunt I would do a 200-mile week and then a 300-mile week and then a 400-mile week and then a 500-mile week, so that my body got used to doing multi-day long rides. In the end, I did quite a few 200-mile weeks, but for various reasons, none of them particularly good – didn't manage the others.

My big ambition was to lose some weight. I was in my mid-60s, 6 foot tall and although not exactly fat, I was certainly carrying some extra ballast, or

[6] Bike Adventures: www.bikeadventures.co.uk

'timber' as we cyclists called it. I had been over 15 stone while working and although I had slimmed down a bit since retiring, I was still on the wrong side of 14 stone and not happy about it. I spoke to my mate Simon, who knew about these things.

'If you like it,' he said, one day as we were out for a ride, 'don't eat it. And if you don't like it, eat it.'

'Is that it?' I said.

'Yep, works every time. And portion size, that's crucial.'

'Butter?'

'Do you like it?'

'Yes.'

'Well then, don't eat it.'

'Crisps? Pizza? Biscuits? Cream? Cake? Ice cream?'

'I think you know the answer, Julian: don't eat it.'

'Where's the joy in that?'

'Your culinary life is over: say goodbye to joy. Joy is off.'

I downloaded a calorie counter app for my phone and started inputting data religiously, counting the calories and ensuring I was in deficit. Although I should have done, I didn't like to weigh myself – having dieted previously, I always found that if I weighed myself and hadn't lost weight or only a pound here or there, I soon got disheartened.

'Don't weigh yourself,' said Simon. 'Go by waist size. If your trousers feel looser, it's working. If they don't, it's not.'

And it worked.

Cycle jerseys that previously struggled to zip up, zipped up with ease; trousers that fought against the button, began to slip down; shirts with tight necks began to show gaps.

'You're looking gaunt,' my wife said, 'are you alright?'

'Yep,' I said, as I started to look like a proper cyclist and less like a fat bloke on a bike.

Coincidentally, a few months before Ian suggested riding LeJog, I had pre-ordered Paul Jones' book[7] about the End-to-End record and it arrived shortly after Ian suggested we ride it. And so, I devoured the book with new eyes. I thought it was wonderful – a superbly written, deeply moving account comprising interviews with many of the surviving record holders, as well as a personal dive into his own personal end to end, his life, loves, work,

---

[7] End to End: The Land's End to John O'Groats Cycling Record by Paul Jones: Little, Brown 2021

insecurities, hopes, fears and dreams. I loved it and made a YouTube video review of it, gushing about how wonderful it was. I manged to send a link to Paul who was touched and thankful and sent me a heartfelt response. Riding the end to end was creeping inexorably and inevitably up my non-existent bucket list.

I was wondering about how to get to Penzance and then back again from John O'Groats. I phoned Ian.

'Have you seen this about bike boxes on the Bike Adventures website?'

'What about them?'

'If you transport your bike in a box, it must be cardboard, so that it folds down to go in the van. You can't use a normal bike box.' Ian had a Bike Box Alan, a big, solid box on wheels, while I had a SciCon rigid bag, each of which had cost us about £500.

'That's an arse,' said Ian. 'We need a plan.'

I spoke to Ian a few days later about getting back from John O'Groats.

'I've got it: hire car,' he said. 'I'm an Avis preferred customer. Wick or Inverness, bikes in the back, drive to Shroppy, drop me off, you drive to Kent, sorted.'

'Seems like a plan,' I said.

Northern Jon was a mate from the Old Portlians Cycling Club, and we'd started riding regularly together, initially during lockdown on Zwift, racing with our pal Pete who'd moved to Dorset, and then latterly out on the road. Jon was a strong rider, stronger than me, despite the heart bypass operation he'd had some years earlier, and we shared an appreciation of cycling kit, nice bikes, open roads, coffee and all the other good things in life.

I told Jon about my plan to do LeJog, one morning as we sat outside Raifes[8] in West Wickham, our favourite café: Jon with an Americano, hot milk on the side, me with a latte in a tall glass, the plastic wrapper of the Lotus biscuit swaying in the breeze.

'Can I help?' he said.

'You could give me a lift to Penzance,' I said, wondering how I was going to get there for the start.

'Let me see,' he said. 'Annabel and I have some friends down that way; maybe we could combine it with that. I'll let you know.'

I hadn't meant my comment seriously (honest!), but this seemed like a brilliant solution and would save me getting the train from Paddington, which would

---

[8] Raifes, 5 Red Lodge Road, West Wickham BR4 0EL, Tel: 020 87778466

no doubt be a faff, with bike and suitcase and rucksack.

I continued riding regularly with Jon – not exactly a training plan, but regular rides of 50 miles or so, often out through the Surrey lanes on routes he'd done a hundred times – Box Hill, Leith Hill, Ranmore Common, Headley, Little Flanders, all the climbs and always a stop for coffee and snacks – cake if we'd ridden hard, cake if we hadn't.

A few weeks before LeJog was due to start I spoke to him.

'Um,' I said, 'not hassling and no problem if you can't, just wondered if you and Annabel had organised anything?'

'No,' he said, 'it didn't work out. But I'll still take you.'

'Wow, you sure?'

'Of course; I said I would, so I will.'

I was touched. And grateful. I'm not keen on trains, at least during a pandemic, even though I know I should be.

*

A couple of years earlier I had started making videos and posting them on YouTube. They were primarily, but not exclusively, about cycling, and some of them proved to be very popular, including one – 7 Reasons Not to Buy a Gravel Bike – which had garnered over 150,000 views. As a result, in October of 2020, my channel became 'monetised' and I qualified for advertising revenue – the more views my videos got, the more money I would earn. I did not expect to make more than a few pounds from them, so decided to give any money I earned to charity.

Two members of the Old Portlians – Michael and Catherine Fowler– were volunteers at a food bank – The Vine[9] - run by the Salvation Army, in New Addington near Croydon. I had spoken to Michael and Catherine about their work there, and so decided to give any money I earnt to The Vine. As some of my videos had garnered quite a lot of views, by June 2021 I had been able to donate over £1500.

I made various videos about my preparations for LeJog, including which bike to ride, which shoes to wear, which socks to bring and then a couple of weeks before the trip was due to start, I made and posted a video entitled 7 Reasons Why I'm Not Doing LeJog.

Jon phoned me.

'What's going on?' he said. 'You're not going?'

---

[9] The Vine food bank:
https://www.justgiving.com/fundraising/newaddingtonsalvationarmy

'Watch the video,' I said. 'It's not that I'm not doing it, it's 7 reasons why I'm not doing it.'

'I'm confused,' said Jon.

'Watch the video.'

My reasons were:

<u>I wasn't doing it for charity</u>

I was, and am, full of admiration for people who undertake challenges for charity and, as it turned out, about half a dozen of the riders in our group were raising money for charity, and very worthy charities they were. My issue was, and is, that people always do things that they want to do and then ask other people to pay for them to do it. And I don't understand why one always had to <u>do</u> something – a walk, a ride, a run, a climb, a row – why can't I spend a week in the Greek islands and raise money for charity that way? Surely, it's just as valid and the charity doesn't care.

I would much prefer to raise money for charity by doing something that I DID NOT WANT TO DO, like voting Tory (which I have never done, and cannot conceive of any circumstance in my lifetime or yours that would cause me to do so); or being a speech writer for Michael Gove; or working as a Chartered Accountant for a week; or even (Heaven forfend) working as Prince Andrew's valet for a day, at his beck and call for 24 hours, ready to service his every whim, squeeze his toothpaste and polish his glasses. Can you imagine being a butler to the least of the least Royals, a man more sinning than sinned against? Not me – but if it's for charity…

## I wasn't doing it because it was on my bucket list

I don't have a bucket list, I don't believe in bucket lists; bucket lists, to me, don't make any sense unless you've got a terminal illness and have been given a timescale, in which case, maybe… I was talking to my friend Mark about this, and he said it might be different if you knew when you were going to go, and I said, 'what would it change if you knew?' and he was stumped. And it got me thinking – maybe one should have that conversation with oneself, and when you've identified a few things – do them. But I still didn't think LeJog would be high on it, or even on it at all.

## I wasn't doing it for the 'challenge'

I'm not trying to push the envelope or stretch myself or find my private Everest. I'm a fit(ish) cyclist, I've done long rides, I've done multi-day rides. Do I think I can't do it? No. Do I think I'll want to quit halfway through? No. Do I think it's too much for me? No. (I may be wrong of course; I guess I'll find out).

## I wasn't doing it to find myself

I'm 65 now and I found myself a few years ago. And, overall, I liked what I found. Yes, I can be quite sarcastic, and I take the piss a lot and I'm always moaning about stuff (like most old people), and I tend to speak too soon which can get me into trouble, but generally it's all done with love in my heart. I try and live a decent life, and I don't always succeed, but at 65 I think the clay is pretty much set and the pot of my life is not too bad. I don't think there's much left to find.

## I wasn't doing it to escape from it all

I have a decent life. I have a wife who loves me, and two fabulous children; I have a roof over my head and enough to eat; I work part time so I have some money coming in and can afford a new bike every year, if necessary (and when isn't it necessary?) and I have a few good friends. I get to cycle a lot, which I enjoy and go to cafes and drink coffee. So, overall, my life is good, and I have no need, and no desire to escape from it. My family might sometimes wish to escape from me, but that's a different matter.

## I was maybe doing it to discover Britain

Over the last few months, I'd made a few trips to parts of Britain I hadn't seen before.

I met up with Ian in Malvern in Worcestershire and we'd spent a couple of days cycling in the Malvern Hills and visiting Monmouth, Hereford, Evesham, Upton on Severn, and riding in the Wye Valley and up a few tough climbs, including one called Symonds Yat where Ian was knocked off his bike by a shit driver. And I'd spent a weekend in

Derbyshire, staying at my friend Kirstine's Air BnB property in Belper[10], cycling along Sustrans routes and visiting Matlock, Buxton and the plague village of Eyam.

Riding LeJog would give me an opportunity to see some new parts of the country and maybe find some places I'd want to return to.

So, why was I doing it, you ask?

Ultimately, I suppose, I was doing it because Ian asked me, and I didn't have anything else to do, and wasn't quick enough to say no, and who knows, maybe some of the reasons I said I wasn't doing it for, would turn out to be in error. But there was another reason: I remembered Mallory's reply, when asked why he wanted to climb Everest: 'because it's there.' Land's End to John O'Groats is the key ride for a British cyclist to complete – because it's there.

---

10

https://www.airbnb.co.uk/rooms/11319778?translate_ugc=false&federated_search_id=520a60b2-34e6-4a36-8f3e-d02007cbae43&source_impression_id=p3_1631518867_dOlbqXj1FTl%2Fj8ch&guests=1&adults=1

# During

## Saturday 20 August 2021

It was dark, half past 4 in the morning, a thick blackness hung over West Wickham. I waited outside my house like a streetwalker, until Jon came along, slowly, with his lights on in his car, looking for a pick-up.

I opened the door and jumped in.

'Morning,' I said.

'You ready?' he said.

'Ready as I'll ever be,' I said.

We set off. Jon put his foot down in the Volvo, and we sped out through West Wickham, through Croydon, down the A23, and then onto the M25, on and on and on, fast we went, there was no traffic, it was almost deserted, grey and misty in the gloom, but the car ran smoothly, very quickly, very quietly, Jon driving carefully in his shorts and his Rapha T-shirt, me sitting beside.

We chatted for a long time, we hardly stopped, there were no breaks, except for a short pause while I had a wazz at the side of the road and then we met our first red light after 230 miles, and that slowed us down for a little bit, and then on and on we went and into Cornwall. Cornwall was grey, empty, caravan after caravan passed us but the

15

pathways and the streets were deserted, nobody stirring at this still early hour, except for a steady stream of VW campervans trundling down into the Cornish, not sunshine; the Cornish greyness, the Cornish darkness, the Cornish poorness. We headed for Penzance, 'let's push on,' I said, 'why don't we go to Land's End? We can't get into the hotel until 4pm anyway'.

It was half past nine, a Saturday morning when we hit Penzance, and then a little rolling 10-mile section until we pulled into Land's End, waited there at the barrier until the parking attendant let us through, £7 to park in a car park and have a look round this piece of land at the end of the known world.

'I want to park here,' I said, 'not buy it.'

The attendant was unmoved; he had heard that feeble joke too many times before and it washed over him like a surfer's wave.

Land's End is a bleak place; it's not a happy place, it's an entertainment complex with not much entertainment, it's an experience with little to experience; there's a couple of desultory 'gift' shops, a couple of coffee shops, a Cornish pasty place, and an Air Rescue helicopter incongruously parked in the middle of the quadrangle.

There was a meagre exhibition housed near the entrance about the LeJog route, with pictures of some of the people who had done the route and the various methods they had had used, or objects they had taken: pushing a pram, with a door on their head, on penny farthings or tandems and Ian Botham's shoes.

Botham – once a famous cricketer, now a Peer of the Realm – had walked to raise money for Leukaemia and Lymphoma research in 1985 (although he had walked south – John O'Groats to Land's End), and his trainers were reverently displayed in a glass case like a splinter from the true cross or a lock of Princess Diana's hair. They were large shoes, worn and crumpled and the reek of Lord Botham's sweaty feet still oozed through the glass. I stood and drank in the magnificence of his footy walk and those mundane shoes, preserved forever here at the end of the known world. Why only his shoes? Why not socks, a jacket, a stick (if he had one), underpants or a hat, all the accoutrements of his long, long stroll? The label offered no clue.

We went looking for the sign, the iconic sign where you had your photograph taken before you headed off for John O'Groats; we found it eventually, it was on the edge, near the crashing sea, behind a fence, with a little booth beside it.

'Form an orderly queue,' the sign said, 'when you get to the end of the queue, tell the attendant what name you want on the stand.'

And then the attendant would go up to the stand; he'd have a bag of letters hanging from his waist like jailer's keys, and he'd change the letters so that it showed your name or where you'd come from; and then you stood there with a rictus grin deforming your face, arm around your girlfriend or boyfriend, while he took your photograph, and charged you £10. I couldn't see the point of driving to Land's End to have your photo taken next to a sign, so saved my money, but it was a popular event and the queue snaked around the rocky headland in the mist.

Vanessa was at the front of the queue, from Bradford, and she stood in the mist and the drizzling rain, weakly smiling and clutching her iPhone, pointing at the sign which pointed to Bradford as the photographer snapped her picture, and the grey clouds hung over everything like a bad smell.

We didn't stay there, not to take our photograph, but instead we went into the café – a Cornish pasty place – and boy, was that a tasty pasty – hot and meaty and oniony and turnipy and all the other things swedey that the cattle normally eat, and a sausage roll for me while Jon had sausage, chips and beans, 3 sausages to fill him up after his long drive.

And then out of the café, and we saw a path snaking around and down the rocky face, looking out towards the lighthouse, and we followed the path down, past big lumps of boulders, broken steps, broken paving, broken stones, gravel, very few people around, until we got to the edge of the cliff which was roped off. Ten feet below, clinging precariously to the path, we could see a man with his young child, skipping around through the rocks, teetering on the edge, waving to Mummy.

'Why would you do that?' I said to Jon. 'Why would you take a young child there, onto the cliff edge - how can people be so stupid?'

'Ah,' said Jon, 'the kid would have done it anyway.'

'Yes,' I said, 'but that's why we have adults to stop them doing stupid things; they're called parents, you're supposed to look after your children.'

'I suppose so,' said Jon.

We walked on the path and came to a little farm; there was a cat there, 'Land's End Cat' said the tag around its neck. Jon stroked it and took some photographs to feed his Instagram portfolio and then we passed some more animals - alpacas.

'Are they alpacas?' I said. 'Or are they horses; they look much the same. Bovine TB anyway, heading for execution, no doubt.'

And then back up the path, back to the bleak, white-washed building, the faded, empty lost hotel, the cars parked £7 a time, ready to look at Land's End.

'It's not just the end of the land,' I said, 'it's the end of the sea, the end of the ocean, the ocean ends here

where it hits the land and anyway, where is Land's
End, where is the point where it stops, there must
be a foot or a yard-wide area, an inch even, X marks
the spot, why can't we find it?'

'I don't know Julian,' said Jon.

The Land's End experience was tired and
underwhelming, paint peeling from the buildings,
the shops selling rock and knick-knacks, souvenirs
looking a little lost and lonely, but the land itself
was brutal and harsh. There was something
elemental about this hallowed patch of ground,
only famous for its co-ordinates, that raised it above
these lacklustre buildings.

'You can build if you want,' the land seemed to say,
'but we were here before you came and we'll be
here after you've gone, and you can fight if you
want and try and hold back the time and lay down
your shallow roots and charge £7 for parking, but
this land is ours and will still be here long after
you've gone and you'd better remember that.'

I wondered if the ancients had known what this
was. When exactly had people discovered that this
patch of land was the furthest Southwest in the
country? Before that, it was just a place, a rocky
promontory, harsh and cold and forbidding and in
many ways, it still was, despite the desperate
attempts to make it warm and friendly and
inviting, a tourist destination because that's all it
was - a destination.

It started to rain then, with heavy gusts of wind and the rain whipped across the damp gravel, the huddled figures under their collapsing campervan awnings, and Jon and I high tailed it back to the warm car, jumped in and then headed back to Penzance.

*

We pulled into Penzance and found the hotel; it was a white building 3 or 4 storeys high on the sea-front, obviously it had seen better days. Jon backed the car into the carpark, and we looked up at the dark, grey, shuttered windows looking out over the town.

'It looks like a Borstal,' I said, 'reminds me of a time when I was there.'

We went in through the back door and into a hair-dressing salon.

'What is this?' I said. 'I think we took a wrong turning somewhere.'

A woman was cutting another woman's hair, it lay in clumps clustered around the chair; she looked at us, shuffling with suitcases and me with my bike, and jerked her head as if she had done this a thousand times before.

'It's upstairs,' she said, with a sigh.

We went up the stairs and into an echoing empty lobby, deserted except for a young man behind the desk, scrolling through the internet on his computer.

'Yes?' he said.

'We've got a reservation,' I said, 'can we check in, we're a bit early?'

'Ooooooofff,' he said, not looking busy. 'Covid.'

It's always bloody Covid, I thought.

'Little short of staff,' he said, 'I don't know if the rooms will be ready. I'll check with housekeeping, but I doubt if they'll be ready before 4; 3 maybe. If you're lucky.' We didn't feel lucky.

'Could you make it 3?' I asked, 'we're going cycling.'

'Okay,' he said, 'I'll do my best.' And went back to the internet.

'Can we leave our stuff?' I said.

'I suppose so, over there, the library.' He gave us a key. I opened the door to the library – it was full of bits of old furniture, broken lamps, dull paintings of minor dukes, a few wine glasses, a pram, but no books.

We headed out into Penzance. It had stopped raining, but it was still grey, overcast and dull, warm but with a stiff breeze. We walked along a long stretch of sea-front, looking across to St Michael's Mount, standing dark and forbidding like a Tintin castle, away over the choppy sea, vaguely poking through the mist. And then the Jubilee pool, a faded sign, paint peeling and rust streaks in the walls.

'Why is the Queen responsible for so many pools?' I asked Jon. 'Is she a noted swimmer? All these poorly designed public amenities in her name.'

But the pool itself actually looked quite nice and was surprisingly busy; a large, open-air pool and beside it a smaller children's pool with families happily splashing.

'I don't know if it's heated,' I said to Jon.

'Why? You going in?'

'No,' I said.

We walked on, past a war memorial, a wreath of poppies at its base; so many towns, so many lost young people, and into a harbour where there were several rather tired, rusty looking boats. But there were also some nice, interesting ones – a wooden hulled and tall masted schooner that wouldn't have looked out of place in the Bahamas or Antibes, if it had had a lick of paint, a butler with a bottle of champagne and a blonde on the foredeck.

'I never fancied a boat,' I said. 'However much you pay, you've still got a place that's smaller than a studio flat, and it costs a fortune to run. And you'd never use it enough – it would sit there, getting old and worn and tired like the rest of us, but on the water.'

There was a little Swiss Family Robinson type skiff, and a young man with a beard was messing about with the rigging, getting ready to head out and dive for treasure.

We walked along a bit further and then headed uphill back into town and found a bookshop where we browsed, wearing our masks, glasses fogging up, such a 2021 tell-tale sign, hands sanitized against the lurking germs, and then back towards the hotel.

'I need a shit,' I said to Jon.

'Yeah, me too. Shall we go in here?' as we passed a café.

'No,' I said, 'I don't want a public shit in a strange town. Let's go back to the hotel. Maybe we can get a coffee and use their toilet. It might be better.'

So, we went back to the hotel, went inside and found the same young man surfing the same internet.

'Not ready yet,' he said, 'I'll phone house-keeping.' And then pretended to call.

We sat in the deserted lounge looking over the sea and the sun came out and blazed through the window, and it got hotter and hotter, and we moved seats back into the shadows, but the coffee was tasty, and we played with our phones looking at Instagram and sending WhatsApp messages, until we started to drift off into sleep, having been up since 4am, until finally our rooms were ready and we went in, separately, to have a shower.

*

A group of about 8 Bike Adventures riders gathered at 5pm at the Longboat Hotel (the group was split between two hotels) for the ride to Land's End. There was some faffing – bikes were being assembled and checked, while some of the party had not yet arrived, still standing on the train from Paddington, an earlier train having been cancelled, including Kevan, who had paid First Class and stood, trapped between his bike bag and a series of suitcases, as the Covid Express rolled through the English countryside heading west.

David, a youngish rider dressed in black, on a black Cannondale Supersix, had a problem with one of the boa dials on his shoes.

'I just took them out of the bag,' he said. 'It won't tighten.'

Everyone crowded around, offering helpful and unhelpful suggestions until Martin, one of the Ride Leaders, found some black electrical tape and wrapped it around the shoe to hold the dial on.

'Best I can do,' he said. 'You need a new shoe. Or a new boa dial.'

'I never use boas,' said Ian, sagely, when I told him about the excitement later. 'For that very reason.'

Eventually we set off, our little peloton of strangers, through Penzance, into the evening sunshine, along the coast towards Newlyn and then came to a steep and hard climb, made harder by the Range Rover towing a trailer which kept on stopping to allow oncoming cars to squeeze past, forcing us to stop too and curse. The climb was about 15 or 16% for about 4 or 500 metres and, as it happened and although I hate to mention it, I was first to the top, where I waited, slumped over the bars until my heart slowed down and the others arrived.

'Your legs are like pistons,' said David, as he drew beside me.

'Thanks,' I said, 'we'll see how long they last.' But I was pleased.

We continued along the back, rolling roads, heading to Land's End and some more lumpy climbs but nothing too taxing. The group soon broke into separate bands, me at or near the front, others some way off the back. I was at the front with Mike, one of the Ride Leaders.

'The group is split,' I said. 'We should ease off.'

'There's another Ride Leader at the back,' he said. 'He can keep them together.'

I continued, off the front, head down, pushing the pace, David of the broken boa close behind me, clearly a strong rider but content to take his time on this warm-up section.

I was first to arrive at Land's End. The weather had cleared, the sky was blue, the parking attendant had left his sentry post, the car park was emptying, and I stood in front of the Land's End sign and took a selfie and propped my bike by the Start/Finish sign painted on the road and then rode around to the famous sign – the photographer had left but small groups of people stood by the sign and snapped selfies.

John O'Groats – 874 miles.

I was with John, another of the group, slim, mid-40s, old looking bike, a rucksack on his back, who was staying in the same hotel as me. We'd been told that we had to be sitting down for dinner at 7.15 at the other hotel – our hotel's restaurant was closed due to a shortage of staff, and it was now 6.30.

'It's 10 miles,' I said, 'let's TT it back to Penzance.' He grunted and we set off, alternating through and off, like a couple of school-kids on their first bikes, tonking along the A30, past Sennen Cove, the sea on our left, little traffic, through fading light, until we got to the turn-off to Newlyn which I had taken with Jon, and knew that it led to Penzance, while John continued on a different route, and although he'd been in front, I reached the hotel before him, puffing and hanting but glad to be first.

At one point, three quarters done, my heart pounding, I said to John, or shouted over the sound of rushing wheels,

'I've got 950 miles to ride, I'm going to ease off,' but he kept on riding, and so of course I had to give chase.

We got back just after 7, so after a very quick shower and change of clothes, we met up in the lobby to walk the half mile or so to the other hotel.

Ian had arrived in Penzance a couple of days earlier with his wife and had already ridden the Land's End to Penzance section, so while I rode out, he had gone for a walk with Jon and become best buddies, finding they had much in common.

John and I walked swiftly from our hotel to the other; ours was short of staff and the echoing restaurant was closed, acres of tables standing empty, still with their cutlery and glasses laid, abandoned in the night like the Marie Celeste or the Titanic. As I walked, a text pinged on my phone. It was Jon.

'Where are you? Dinner's at 7.30. You'll miss it.' We hurried on.

Dinner was surprisingly tasty – fish and chips and proper peas, not that mushy stuff the northerners eat, while the group gradually met and meshed. We appraised our fellow riders: who would be the fast boys, the slow boys, the 'might not make its', the ones prone to injury or mechanicals, the ones with expensive bikes or cheap bikes, new bikes or old bikes, the ones making videos, the ones doing it for charity or lost loves or to find themselves, the strong, the weak, the old and the young, who would get an injury or give up?

There were two Ride Leaders on this trip – Richard and Martin – and a third rider Mike, who had previously worked as a Ride Leader but was now a paying customer, although he still gave the introductory speech, for reasons I never quite discovered.

'How many times have you ridden this?' I asked him later.

'Eight,' he said, 'this will be ninth. I wanted to do 10 before I was 65.'

Mike gave us an idea of what to expect and spoke a lot about the importance of eating adequately – if we don't eat enough in the first few days, he said, we would not make it.

Our group was in a separate dining area away from the rest of the pub. As we finished eating, a man entered who didn't seem part of our group and started talking about golf.

'What's he on about?' I said to Ian. 'What's this about golf?'

It transpired that the man had walked from John O'Groats for charity, hitting a golf ball all the way, as you do.

'I'm raising money for my charity,' he said, '3 of my friends died recently from heart failure. I'm trying to raise money for defibrillators and to encourage people to get trained in CPR. How many of you can do CPR?'

A few people tentatively put their hands up, like schoolchildren who aren't sure if they know the answer to teacher's question.

I sat up and listened. This was a cause very dear to my heart (no pun intended), as my best friend's daughter had died at the age of 16 from sudden heart failure, and my friend supported the charity CRY – Cardiac Risk in the Young[11].

'Anyway,' said the man, 'I shall go now. But you're undertaking a great adventure; I hope it goes well and I wish you every success.'

The Ride Leaders then handed out Bike Adventures jerseys, luggage labels and route sheets and took some questions. There were a couple of Geordies with impenetrable accents on the trip. One of them asked a question of the Ride Leaders, but I don't

---

[11] CRY: www.c-r-y.org.uk

think they, or anyone else frankly, had the faintest idea of what he was talking about.

Penzance to Land's End to Penzance

Miles: 24.7
Elevation: 1975 ft
Ride time: 1 h 38 m
Average speed: 15.1 mph

*

## Sunday, 21 August 2021

### Penzance, Cornwall to Tavistock, Devon

The big day. I woke up early, about half past 4 and thought I'd get back to sleep but didn't – this was to be pretty much the pattern for the rest of the trip. I lay there, as the first leaks of light shuffled round the curtain, playing with my phone, recording impressions on an Olympus voice recorder I'd bought for that purpose and waiting until I could safely get up.

The big question of the day is: do I go to Land's End this morning and start the ride there, or do I start from Penzance?

The decision I reached is to start from Penzance. Why?

Yesterday I rode from Penzance to Land's End and back to Penzance, so I have done that leg and it's not as if I'm going for the record and trying to do the whole ride non-stop, so what difference does it make that Land's End was yesterday?

In addition, Bike Adventures has hired a coach to take those riders to Land's End who want to go, or got in too late on Saturday to join our group ride, but that won't leave until about 8.45 so it will be about 10 before riders set off from Land's End, and today is supposed to be the toughest day of the trip – 93 miles and 6500 feet of climbing, so adding on that additional leg is not impossible, but it adds an extra bit that I've already done.

I was riding an Orbea Terra, a carbon gravel bike which I had ordered some months previously, but which had only been delivered a couple of weeks earlier.

I had a choice of bikes to ride: a Fairlight Secan – a steel gravel bike with a Shimano 1x gear system, supremely comfortable, but heavy; a Mason Definition, once my forever bike, until I bought another - an aluminium endurance bike with Shimano electronic Di2 which I had ridden with great success and no problems in the Dolomites; a Giant Defy – a carbon endurance bike with Shimano Ultegra, low gears and disc brakes which I had ridden with great success and no problems in the Picos; and a Time Izon – a lightweight carbon road bike with electronic Shimano Di2 and rim brakes.

All these bikes had been serious contenders at one time or another, although I soon (but reluctantly) dismissed the Time as I was now a convert to disc brakes. I had almost settled on the Giant, but it couldn't take mudguards which I thought could be essential, whereas the Orbea could. As it happened, however, the mudguards I bought for the Orbea had an annoying rattle which I couldn't eliminate, so I left them behind.

I ordered an Ass Saver instead; a strip of some plasticky material designed to slot into the saddle that would protect your arse (or ass) from the worst of the spray kicked up by the rear wheel. However, I removed it after the first day – it looked naff and got in the way when I swung my leg over the bike; and in any case, maybe I'd be lucky, and it wouldn't rain.

I did, however, remove the lightweight carbon wheels with 30mm tyres from the Giant and put them on the Orbea, replacing the rather heavy alloy wheels with 38mm gravel tyres which were originally on the Orbea, believing (rightly, as it transpired) that the weight saving would be an advantage.

I'd covered less than 100 miles on the Orbea before setting off on this mammoth journey and on the final ride before we left, I was riding with my friend Simon when I heard a slight but annoying chain rub. We were near FAB Cycle Servicing in Farnborough[12] so we popped in.

'New bike?' said the mechanic, whose name was Craig.

'Yep,' I said.

'Is it booked in for a 6-week service? Bike shops should offer that.'

'No,' I said. 'I got it online.'

---

[12] FAB Cycle Servicing, 141 high Street, Farnborough, Kent BR6 7AZ
www.fabcycleservices.com Tel: 01689 490922

'Interesting,' said Craig. 'You ought to.'

He put the bike in the stand and started fiddling.

'Cable stretch,' he said, after about a minute of tweaking, 'always happens with a new bike. All sorted.'

'I'm doing LeJog,' I said. 'Friday.'

'Have you checked the bolts?'

'Um, yeah, I attached the handlebars and that.'

'Interesting,' said Craig, mysteriously, fetching a neat looking digital torque wrench.

'Oh, dear oh dear,' he said, tutting. 'The thing is these carbon bikes are built to such tight tolerances now that you have to check the bolts regularly. Your stem bolts aren't right. You don't want the handlebars slipping on some descent, now do you?'

'Er, no,' I said. 'Thanks.'

We left the hotel at 8.45 – Ian, me, John and David of the Cannondale Super Six and the broken boa, sticky electrical tape enveloping his shoe like a bandage and Jon waved us off and took some photos. There had been a certain amount of faffing – waiting for the coach, loading the coach, rounding up stragglers, and a rider named Roy who asked if anyone had any anti-inflammatory tablets as he was suffering from some ailment or other. I had a packet of Nurofen and offered it to him, thinking he'd take two. He took the packet of 8.

'Er, don't take them all,' I said. 'Drug-taking is not allowed on this trip.'

'I'll buy you some,' said Roy, 'when I get to a chemist.'

We rolled along the promenade towards the other hotel where there was a track pump. Everyone pumped up their tyres and then pumped them again, in case they'd missed a bit, and I purchased a spare inner tube from Martin, one of the ride leaders – did I have a premonition?

We saw two of the group – Craig and Chris – who were saying goodbye to their wives. There were tearful hugs in the street as if they were heading off to war and the troop train was waiting impatiently on the platform, and then the wives turned away, wiping their eyes and looking forlorn, and waved from their cars as their menfolk slowly rode away on their big adventure.

We headed off along the coast road on a beautiful day, the sky a hazy shade of blue with few cloud streaks and a warm sun, the roads flat and quiet, St Michael's Mount hovering in the haze to our right, a scaled down version of Mont St Michel just over the water.

I was in front, the route a breadcrumb trail unscrolling on my Wahoo, the bike feeling comfortable and fast, my legs were strong, and all was right with the world. After a few miles we turned inland, away from the shining sea towards Redruth, as the road began to climb, and the hills gradually revealed themselves. Ian's Garmin showed how many categorised climbs there were and as we hit the first notable hill, he called out,

'This is number 1 of 17.'

The climbs were generally fairly short – half a mile maximum – and fairly steep but not that steep, 10% up to 15%, but nothing particularly horrid and leg-breaking. I had expected worse – the Ride Leaders and others had said that the first two days through Cornwall and Devon were the worst with brutal 25% climbs and a constant rolling route, but…but… I didn't find it so.

It may have been the bike – lightweight and new with a 48/31 chain-set and a 11-34 cassette; it may have been me – newly slim and looking close to a real cyclist's physique; it may have been the riding I'd done and the strength in my legs; it may have been that the route was not as bad as it could have been; or maybe it was a bit of all four, mixed with the excitement of this iconic ride on the bumpy narrow road to the deep north.

The pitted tarmac unspooled ahead of us like a worn C90 cassette tape, as our little peloton tapped out a steady rhythm.

I was on the front, but John generally came past me on the climbs – I was taking it reasonably steady, not pushing the effort, trying to stay within myself, not something I'm generally good at, always wanting to prove something to someone else or me. Ian went at his own pace, solid but steady, legs moving like a metronome, behind us but he always got there in the end with little wasted effort, the months of training on his flash Stages bike paying off.

I was riding along, David just behind me until he drew alongside.

'Vittoria Corsa's?' he said.

'Yep, tan wall, 30mm, look the dog's bollocks.'

'You're brave,' he said.

I was suddenly suspicious.

'Brave? What do you mean, brave?'

'Oh, you know.'

'No, I don't know. What?'

'They have a reputation,' said David. 'Not exactly puncture proof.'

'They've been okay so far', I said, defensively, riding away from this bearer of bad news.

And then after 30 miles, I couldn't believe it – a puncture in the Vittoria's and in my Tubolito tube!

The Tubolito was a bright orange thermo-plastic inner tube, quite new to market, significantly lighter and smaller than a butyl tube and supposedly more puncture proof. I'd bought some, planning to put them in my saddlebag to save weight, but before setting off on this trip had decided to put them in my tyres, on the basis that unless I used them, I'd never know if they were any good or not. And they weren't. The support van came along just as I was changing the tyre and had a track pump – although not a very good one – but I used that to pump the tyre. It was easy enough changing the tube, and heaven knows, I'd done it enough times in the past, but it was still frustrating and annoying to get one so soon – although I was grateful that I had purchased that additional tube before setting off from Penzance.

We continued, the road winding through a wooded area and up a steep climb, and then turning sharp left. David had disappeared off the front, Ian was just behind, and I looked around and there was no sign of John. David, Ian and I had the route on our Garmins or Wahoo's, but John, being old school and more careful with his money, was using the yellow printed sheets with the route guidance which the Ride Leaders had handed out at the pre-ride briefing. I shouted out.

'John!'

And then again,

'John!'

And then again, and louder,

'JOHN!'

And then again, my hand cupped around my mouth to boost the sound,

**'JOHN!!'**

My hoarse shouty voice echoed through that wooded emptiness but there was no responding shout.

'What's happened to him?' I said to Ian.
'Dunno,' he said.

'You don't care, do you?' I said accusingly.

He shrugged and made ready to set off, as John came slowly round the bend and up the hill.

'I was shouting, man,' I said. 'Where were you?'

'I stopped. Take some photos.'

We continued through these narrow, rutted, leaf strewn back roads of Cornwall until we rounded a bend and came upon a farm shop and café called Cows and Sows.

'Who's for coffee?' I said. 'Looks nice.'

'Me,' said John.

'What about David?' said Ian.

'He's gone,' I said.

'He'll think we've had a problem,' said Ian.

A farmer's wife in an apron stuck her head out of the door.

'Are you coming in?' she said.

'We're arguing,' I said. 'Can't decide.'

She disappeared back inside the inviting café.

'I'm going on,' said Ian.

Reluctantly, John and I clipped in and followed him, away from the aroma of latte, home-made cakes, cows and sows. We didn't see David for the rest of the day.

We rode on and reached Fraddon, where there was an enormous retail park with a TK Maxx and a Marks and Spencer which had a wrap-around café upstairs, with an open-air terrace looking over the fields and valleys towards the sea, where we stopped. A steady stream of people wandered in and out, which made me think that maybe people in Cornwall didn't go to the beach for a day out –

after all they lived there – but instead followed the tourist trail to Marks and Sparks for underpants and bras, garlic bread and ready meals, and a coffee and a cake on the terrace with some sweaty long-distance cyclists.

It must have been a busy day as the shelves were almost bare – egg mayonnaise sandwiches (it's always egg mayonnaise) seemed to be the only food left, together with crisps and the ubiquitous carrot cake. I was concerned that this being our first stop and the pickings meagre, I might struggle to get the required nutrition each day – 5000 to 6500 calories were probably needed and that is very difficult to eat in a day (for most people anyway).

We ate and drank and basked in the hot sunshine and then headed off again, down a long sweeping descent, crossed the Tamar – the border between Cornwall and Devon (although I only found that out later) - and then inevitably a long climb up the other side, away from the river before finally dropping down into Tavistock.

The group was split between two hotels again, with John, Ian and I all billeted in the Bedford Hotel, which seemed a fine, old, large traditional hotel resembling a public school. It was very busy and the very nice lady on reception who led us to our rooms said it had re-opened in May and had been full every night since, which seemed a stroke of good fortune after the year they must have had.

My room was very pleasant and spacious, and I spent the first 15 minutes connecting my phone, Wahoo and lights to the charging ports, loading Strava and naming my ride, before stripping off and plunging my sweaty kit into the basin to soak and finally having a shower and dressing for dinner. This was to be the evening ritual every day for the rest of this ride.

At 7pm I went down to the bar which was very busy but there was no sign of Ian. I ordered a gin and tonic at the bar.

'What sort of gin do you want?' said the barman. I didn't know there were different gins – well, I did, but I'd only ever drunk Gordon's in the green bottle, so I said that would do. I am a creature of habit.

I sat at a table next to the bar, watching and listening. Two attractive, well-dressed young ladies came up to the bar.

'11 Sambuca shots,' said one of them, in a white filmy dress, who looked about 19, waving a credit card in her hand. The barman, masked, looked at her closely but didn't ask for any ID.

'I don't think I've got 11,' he said, 'I'll need to open another bottle.'

The women stood together chatting, one waving her black credit card – Tavistockracy on a night out.

The barman looked at me, the look that men give each other when they see an attractive woman.

At that moment, a dog snuffling at the feet of its owner in another part of the bar, started barking, loudly and raucously and irritatingly. This barking continued intermittently for all the rest of the time we were in the bar. When it wasn't barking, it was shuffling around the room, alternately sniffing at crotches and eating scraps of food which the other punters flung in its direction.

Ian arrived and I bought him a beer and we sat at the table, becoming more and more irritated at the barking dog.

'A dog,' said Ian. 'A fucking dog. In a bar. Barking. Shouldn't be allowed.'

'Let it go,' I said.

'I can't,' said Ian, which proved to be the most common exchange between us for the rest of the week, although not always in relation to dogs.

A large group of well-dressed young and old people swanned in and out of the restaurant next door and we could hear raucous singing and lots of toasting, presumably of sambuca shots.

'Wedding party,' said Ian, sagely, who knew about these things.

I studied the menu. It was country house posh, with lots of celeriac and foam, drizzle and rocket, pomegranate and tender stem broccoli, truffle shavings, sourdough flakes, jus, reductions, chef's specials, vegan choices – I'm sure all very tasty and lovingly produced – but not what I wanted after 10 hours hard cycling. I wanted pasta or rice or potatoes; some bulk, some plain simple fair and lots of it, not a poncey taster menu of the best of local Devon produce.

'Indian,' said Ian, suddenly. 'We passed one on the way in.'

'Indian?' I said, 'are you sure? Before a big ride tomorrow, is that a good idea?'

'Trust me,' said Ian, 'it's what we need.'

Bike Adventures had booked a table for 7.30 in the hotel restaurant, but we spoke to the receptionist and said we wouldn't be dining in the hotel.

'I'll need to tell Chef,' she said.

'Chef's just opened the tin,' I said to Ian as we left. 'He'll be disappointed.'

We walked up through the quiet town to the Indian restaurant.

'Table for two?' I said, as we pushed open the door.

The waiter showed us to a table, but behind my chair was a curtain and beyond that the door to the street, which was open. A sharp, cold breeze blew across my neck.

'I can't sit here,' I said to Ian, 'it's cold.'

The waiter rather reluctantly showed us to a 4-seat table deeper into the restaurant.

The service was quite slow and, unusually for an Indian restaurant, they didn't bring us poppadums straight-away and we sat there, for what seemed an age, Ian nursing his Kingfisher and me my Diet Coke, until the waiter finally returned.
We ordered a vast array of dishes which came eventually on a weighed down trolley and covered the table – rice and meats, aubergine, okra, dahl, naan breads for bulk, biryanis and reams of poppadums – more food, as it turned out than either Ian or I could consume; until we sat, replete and stuffed with our hot napkins to wipe our hands and Indian detritus spread on the tablecloth like a massacre in the Khyber Pass.

'I think I've got a slow puncture,' said Ian, as we walked back to the hotel. 'I'll need to replace the tyre in the morning. It's a pain.'

Penzance to Tavistock

Miles: 84.5
Elevation: 7887ft
Ride time: 6h 38m

Average speed: 12.7mph

\*

## Monday, 22 August 2021

## Tavistock, Devon to Wookey Hole, Somerset

I went for a little walk before breakfast and took a few photos. There was a plaque on the wall beside the hotel entrance, explaining that the building had originally been built as a residence for the agent of the Duke of Bedford. I reflected on the fact that the duke must have been a very wealthy and successful entertainer in his day, if his agent could afford such a house.

I met John outside, heading off in a hurry.

'Where are you going?' I said.

'I want to get a postcard,' he said.

'Postcard?' I said, 'can you still buy such things? Do people still send postcards?'

'I do,' he said. 'I think it's nice to send and receive postcards. It's for my daughter, she's 11. I'm going to send her one from every stop. Much better and more personal than a text message.'

Which I thought was a very sweet thing to do and said so in a WhatsApp message to my daughter.

One thing you really appreciate if you undertake LeJog, is just how much an achievement it is for those riders who undertake to break the record. Achieving the record has long been a 'thing' and almost as soon as the bike was invented, the first riders set a record on a Penny Farthing. At the time we rode it - August 2021 - the male record was held by Mike Broadwith in a time of 43 hours 25 minutes 13 seconds, set on 17 June 2018, and the female record had only just been broken by Christina Mackenzie, in a time of 51 hours 5 minutes 27 seconds, which she set on 30 July 2021, only 3 weeks previously.

To think that the record was well under 48 hours, and we had already been going for 10 hours and had only reached a short way into Devon! And we thought we were going well! Our average speed for that first (full) leg – Penzance to Tavistock – was 12.7 mph, while the average speed of those record breakers was over 20mph, hour after soul-numbing hour after mind playing tricks hour after hallucinating hour for the whole duration!

It was also strange to think that in a few days we would be in the Lake District, and in less than a week we would be in Scotland, which just goes to show that if you keep on pedalling you can cover enormous distances.

Reflecting on Sunday's ride, I didn't find it all that difficult, which I attributed to a few reasons:

- I'm quite fit and more importantly, have lost over a stone in weight which makes a tremendous difference if you're climbing
- The bike is quite light with low gears

- We took it at a sensible pace, weren't trying to race and rode within ourselves (well, I did anyway). And if John raced away from me on some of the climbs – which he did – I let him go and didn't chase after him, which in other situations I probably would have done
- The climbs were not as hard as I was expecting – some were 14, 15 or 16% but I anticipated 18, 19 or even 20% and we didn't have that.

We left the Bedford Hotel after a tasty, full English breakfast at 8.30am, travelled a few hundred metres and went straight into a climb which lasted for about a mile, before it eased off and then started again and seemed to go on and on, the scenery becoming barer and more desolate until we reached what seemed to be the top of Dartmoor. I pulled into a carpark which a few of the other riders had also reached and was greeted with a fabulous view stretching across and down the wild wilds of Dartmoor in every direction, the mist hanging over Tavistock, which was nestled far below us, scattered sheep resting peacefully on the open land.

I saw later on the BBC news, that a police rescue team, out searching for a teenager who was suffering from hypothermia, had stumbled across the lifeless body of a cyclist somewhere in the Dartmoor wilderness; cause of death unknown but probably an accident due to hitting a rock on a gravel trail. Looking around, one could well understand how someone could lose their life and not be found for days in this wilderness.

We weren't quite at the top but had a bit more climbing to do, before reaching the summit where we saw Martin and the support van. Ian stopped to grab his gilet for the descent; it was pleasantly warm but there was a strong headwind (which proved the weather feature for every day of this trip), which could turn cold on a fast drop.

'Look out for Dartmoor Prison,' said Martin, 'it'll be on your right.'

After a long descent we started to climb again, first through a wooded section and then out onto open moorland, where we saw a sign:

SHEEP LYING ON ROAD

I spoke to the first sheep I saw.

'You're a sheep, aren't you?'

'No, I'm not,' said the sheep, with a distinct Devon burr in its voice.

'Yes, you are,' I said, 'don't lie to me,'

'I'm not,' said the sheep, 'straight up, I'm not.'

'What are you then?'

'An alpaca,' said the sheep.

'Well, in that case, it's off to the slaughterhouse for you, matey.'

'Okay,' said the sheep, sheepishly, 'I'm a sheep.'

There were also several fearsome looking cattle with long sharp horns, that were standing half on the verge, half in the road, partially blocking it and giving every indication of preparing to charge. Cars had stopped, afraid to drive through them and provoke a stampede but I rode on carefully and unthreateningly, pointing my GoPro at them and filming as we glided through. They were clearly used to being photographed and left us alone.

Distracted by the lying sheep and the fearsome cows, I failed to spot Dartmoor Prison and so missed waving to some old friends.

Not long after, I had my second puncture of the trip! I couldn't believe it! And it was the other Tubolito tube. I was incensed. Richard, one of the Ride Leaders who was on ride duty that day – he alternated riding and driving with Martin – arrived on his bike with a big frame pump to assist.

It took us about 3 hours to do the 30 miles to Crediton. John was not with us; he obviously having decided that our pace the day before was not enough for him, and David had found another peloton, so Ian and I formed our own little team.

'We'll have something to eat in Crediton, and then stop in Debiton and go to the toilet,' I said to Ian.

He gave me a sideways look.

'How long have you been thinking of that joke?' he asked.

'Tavistock,' I said, 'or possibly Penzance.'

Crediton had a pleasant market square and we settled down for some snackage, as Ian called it.

Ian went to one coffee shop and ordered coffees, but they didn't have any food – the rest of our group had presumably eaten all the pies and the cakes. I went to another café to get some food. 'Where are you sitting?' said the woman behind the counter.

I pointed to the table where we had left our things.

'You can't sit there,' she said, pointedly, 'they're not our tables. They belong to the other café.' I sensed a café rivalry was being played out.

'It's okay,' I said, 'we're getting coffee from the other place.'

She gave me a funny look.

'It'll have to be take-away then,' she said, again pointedly.

I returned to our table where Ian had arrived with the coffee, which was delicious. Eventually, after a long wait, my food arrived – a polystyrene box with a smoked salmon bagel inside, a small patch of salad, a few tortilla chips (4 I think), and a plastic fork; and a scone with butter which came in a plastic bag, like you might use for your dog's faeces.

Someone from the group had placed a message on the WhatsApp group saying there was a bike shop in the town, so after finishing my food, I walked there (it proved to be further away than expected) and bought a spare tube and some Torq energy bars.

There were 10 categorised climbs on today's route showing on Ian's Garmin but most of those came within the first 30 or 40 miles. We left Crediton at 1.45 and still had about 70 miles to go – it was going to be a late one!

We left in the company of Mark and Charlie, a father and son pairing who I immediately christened Batman and Robin. Charlie had a Garmin but for some reason it kept on sending them off course so that they covered more miles than anyone else – Mark was using his phone but didn't have the course loaded on that, and so they had become more and more lost, only reaching Crediton by a lucky accident after going several miles off course.

Richard, one of the Ride Leaders, and Emma, the sole female in the group, had also arrived at Crediton sometime after us, so our little 6-person peloton set off together. However, that peloton did not last long as Richard and Emma soon slipped behind and then Mark and Charlie couldn't quite decide if they were fast enough to keep up with Ian and I (they weren't) or were as slow as Richard and Emma (which they weren't either), and so lingered somewhere in no-man's land.

Ian and I knew that Richard and Emma would catch them and show them the way – if they didn't take a wrong turning – and so we pressed on until we reached Taunton and a new county – Somerset.

We passed a Costa Coffee in the centre of town and Ian and I paused for a snack. I ordered a Wiltshire ham and cheddar cheese toastie with tea for both of us.

I said to the lady behind the glass screen behind the counter,

'Do you take American Express?'

'It's take-away, really,' she said, which I thought was an odd response.

'No,' I said, 'do you take American Express?'

Maybe she had a problem with my accent as she replied,

'Normally, we prefer customers to carry their own food.'

I was distinctly nonplussed and wondered where this surreal conversation was likely to end up.

I held the card up to her vizor behind the screen behind the counter and tried again.

'Do you take American Express?' I asked in a loud, but I hoped not rude, Fawlty Towers type voice.

'Yes,' she said, ignoring the rest of our lost conversation.

I tapped. One of the main economic and social changes as a result of Covid is the obsolescence of cash. Every place we stopped at took payment by contactless card, and Ian, who is well up on these things, always used his phone to pay, and in fact didn't carry any cards.

I took my water bottles and went into the toilet to fill them up, but the basin was too shallow, and the taps wrongly angled so that I couldn't get the mouth of the bottles under the flow of water, except almost horizontally, so of course the water flowed in and then flowed out again. As I came out of the toilet, I saw Mark who had just arrived.

'They'll do them at the counter,' he said. 'It's a rule; places have to give you water.'

However, there was a long queue, so I reached behind the glass screen and took a paper coffee cup and went back into the toilet and used that to fill my bottle.

When I went back outside, I saw that Richard and Emma had arrived. Emma's Garmin was running low on charge and although she had a power bank, she had brought the wrong lead and so couldn't charge her Garmin. I had a spare lead for my Wahoo and so lent her mine.

Mark and Charlie were sitting at the table.

'Batman and Robin?' said Mark, looking at me.

'You told them?!' I said to Ian.

'Truth will out,' he said, like a Shakespearean actor, 'honesty is the best policy.'

'Actually, we like it,' said Mark.

Ian and I set off again, still with some 40 miles to go. Luckily, thereafter it was pretty much flat all the way, with only some minor climbs and so we fair tonked along.  Eventually we reached the Somerset levels.

'It's pretty flat here,' said Ian.

'It's not called the Somerset Levels for nothing,' I said.

The countryside was glorious, with flat, endless fields and narrow, well-maintained roads set at right angles to each other, hardly any cars and the setting sun skipping through the trees and lengthening the shadows as the cloudless sky turned a deeper hue of blue. We seemed to keep turning left at junctions and all the landscape looked the same.

'I'm sure we've seen this before,' I said to Ian, convinced we were lost.

We crossed a small stone bridge over a stream and looking to my right I saw three cows standing in the water, up to their knees (do cows have knees?), udders dangling in the water, and happily splashing in the water, looking like three middle aged ladies bathing in the Ganges. One was wearing a rubber ring, one had a snorkel and the third had a ball and was trying, unsuccessfully it seemed, to interest the others in a game of water polo.

'I'm stopping,' I said to Ian, 'photo time.'

I took out my phone and took some photos and then took my GoPro from the top tube bag and started filming.

Nearby, a young man had parked his car and was leaning on the fence with a wistful, faraway look in his eye, patting the cows that hadn't gone in the water on the head, or maybe they had already finished their swim.

'Are these your cows?' I asked, by way of conversation.

'No,' he said, 'no, I've just come out for a drive, I like it, I like it around here.'

'You ever see cows in a river before?' I asked.

'No,' he said, 'no, no, no I don't think so.'

'Do you know where Glastonbury is?' I said.

'About 10 miles away,' he said. 'Are you going there?'

'No,' I said, 'I was just curious really. We're on our way to John O'Groats.'

'Have a good trip,' he said.

'Enjoy the cows,' I said.

'They'll be in the Cowlympics,' I said to Ian, later, 'couple of years, you wait and see.'

'You're not wrong,' said Ian.

A few miles further on we found our way blocked by a piece of thin tape strung across the road. A man in wellington boots and wearing a hat was leading some cows across the road and into a field. He carried a slight looking plastic stick or switch in his hand and occasionally tapped a cow on the buttocks if it was moving too slowly or not at all.

Ian and I dismounted and waited.

'Nice to see cows going into a field,' said Ian, who knew about these things.

'Where else would they be?' I said, not knowing about these things.

'In the stalls,' said Ian.

'Front stalls?' I said, 'back stalls? Two four pennies please, front stalls. Or circle, two seats in the circle.'

Both Ian and the farmer ignored me.

'Come along Banknote,' said the farmer, lightly swatting a cow on its bum.

'Banknote?' I said, 'is that its name.'

'Yes,' said the farmer.

'Do they all have names?' I asked.

'Some do, some don't,' he said, mysteriously I thought.

'We saw some in the river, is that common?' I asked.

'We had one in the ditch earlier on,' said the farmer, who may have mis-heard me.

'There was a couple actually, in the river,' I said.

61

'Come on!' shouted the farmer, I think to the cows, 'they're only bicycles, you know what bicycles are.'

'Do they?' I said. 'Come on boys, girls, girls, they are girls, aren't they" I said.

'I know what you mean about keeping them inside,' said the farmer, responding to Ian's earlier point and ignoring my contribution, 'the trouble is, everything in this world boils down to that.' And he made a gesture rubbing his two fingers together. 'We live in a country where people want cheap food.'

'And milk prices haven't gone up, for how long?' said Ian.

'I left school 40 years ago and went to work on a dairy farm and we were getting 15p a litre for milk. We get about 30p now. If you put it through an inflation calculator, we should be getting 65-70p a litre. But the cost of producing it – come on! - just goes up. Come on, if you're quick.'

There was a gap in the cow train, so the farmer lifted the tape, and we rode on.

'Thanks,' I called back.

'Cowlympics and now cowconomics,' I said to Ian, 'I learnt something.'

A short distance further on, a blue Range Rover passed me, a bit close I thought. For once, Ian was ahead, and I heard shouting. The car had stopped, and Ian was speaking to the passenger, a large-girthed man with a florid face.

'A metre and a half,' said Ian, 'you're supposed to leave a metre and a half if you're passing cyclists.'

The large, florid faced man made no response.

'Fuck off, you cunt,' said a large woman who was driving.

The man pressed his window button and the darkened glass rose and sealed them in as it sped off down the road.

'Wankers,' said Ian.

'Let it go mate,' I said.

'I can't,' said Ian, 'you know I can't.'

Five or so miles before arriving at Wookey Hole, the screen on my Wahoo suddenly faded and disappeared and the machine stopped working. I called to Ian, stopped the bike and tried to turn it off and on, but the screen stayed mockingly dark. I fumbled for my phone in my pocket and paged to Strava and set it to record the last of the ride, but now had no breadcrumb route to light my way and relied on Ian. Although I had a charger in my bar bag, of course I had no cable, having lent it to Emma.

We were nearing Wookey Hole and I'd seen a WhatsApp message on my phone at Taunton from Martin about a ford which we would need to cross, and how we should dismount and walk across the footbridge as heavy rain had made the crossing dangerous.

Before I realised where we were, we rounded a bend and there was the ford straight ahead. Ian, who paid as little attention to traffic warnings as he did to traffic lights, stop signs, zebra crossings and most other elements of the highway code, carried straight on and rode through the ford. I hesitated about following him and then carried on, but I had lost momentum when I waited and was therefore forced to pedal before I was halfway across the fast-flowing water. Naturally, that sent my feet into a foot or more of water and the greeny wetness overflowed my shoes and reached almost to my knees. I had visions of toppling over into this watery chasm and drowning here far from home, having ridden the best part of a couple of hundred miles with a Wahoo that didn't work and two punctures in my tubolitos.

Luckily, there were no hidden potholes or large rocks lurking beneath this tsunami, so I reached the other side safely and still moving, albeit slowly and wringing wet.

It was about 7.15 by the time we reached Wookey Hole, an odd place with a series of visitor attractions built around some spectacular caves which I remembered visiting as a child.

We weren't certain where we were staying so rode into the village and saw a place called the Wookey Hole Inn, which looked likely. We were both tired and Ian stayed outside with the bikes while I went inside looking for a receptionist or anything that looked like other cyclists. There were people dining and some people standing at the bar with a single barmaid struggling to serve them, so it took some time before I could attract her attention.

'Er,' I said, 'where can we check in?'

'Wrong place,' she said. 'We've seen loads of your lot, you want the hotel, it's over the road, where that big car park is.'

It was close to dark now and the car park was large and gloomy, but we finally found the hotel beyond the car park, a large nondescript low building resembling a barracks. Martin was outside with the van, gesticulating.

'Dinner is booked for 7.30,' he said, 'you'll have to hurry. If you're lucky they might serve until 8. Take your bikes in your rooms. Captain Jacks.'

'Christ,' said Ian and I together.

The reception area was a forest of wood panelling with a dark and empty bar area next to it.

We grabbed our room keys and found our rooms, very different from the studied elegance of the Bedford Hotel in Tavistock. This was like student accommodation, with threadbare carpet and job lot furniture, but the bed was a double and the water was hot. I upended my suitcase and found some fresh clothes, ran a basin of hot water, added some travel wash and shoved in my shorts and jersey, stripped off and stood under the shower briefly, before hurriedly dressing and heading out to find something to eat.

I had put the Wahoo on to charge and tried saving the remaining part of my ride on Strava on my phone, but the phone froze and when I tried to turn it off, nothing happened.

I met Ian outside.

'Where's the restaurant?' he said.

'I don't know,' I said.

'I thought Martin told you where to go,' he said.

'He did,' I said, 'but I can't remember.' I was tired and had difficulty concentrating and seemed unable to remember what Martin had told me only a few moments before.

'My phone doesn't work,' I said, 'I can't turn it off.'

'Leave it,' said Ian, 'we'll sort it when we're in the restaurant, if we ever find it.'

It was pitch dark now and we were disoriented in that echoing carpark.

I tried to turn my phone off, but nothing happened and instead it started to dial an emergency number; the French emergency services came up on the screen.

'Yes,' said a voice, 'what is your emergency?' He spoke perfect English, for some reason. Maybe he knew it was me.

'I don't have an emergency,' I said, 'I can't turn my phone off. Sorry.'

'Do you want me to end the call at this end?' said the voice.

'Yes,' I said.

I tried to end the call and turn the phone off again and again it phoned France.

Ian and I were blundering round in the car park, trying to see the lights of a restaurant but there was nothing visible in that inky blackness.

A car came along, and Ian stepped into the road and flagged it down, his 6'4" frame in shorts looming out of the gloom. A woman rolled down her window.

'We're looking for Captain Jacks,' he said, 'do you know where it is?'

'Er, no,' she said, backing away from Ian.

Another car came along.

'Captain Jacks?' she shouted as the car rolled past.

'Over there,' came a voice.

'Thanks,' Ian shouted, and we crossed the road, heading towards a darkened building. We found a lighted doorway and Ian peered inside. There was someone there.

'Captain Jacks?' he said, 'is this it?'

'No,' said the woman. 'Follow this building around through that gate, under the archway, it's in the corner, you'll see the sign.'

We went where she pointed, me still clutching my useless dead phone.

We walked through an archway, along a path and passed a kind of child's version of the Black Pearl with models of pirates looking like Johnny Depp or with impossibly large bosoms, earrings and knowing winks, to give the Dads some fun while the children gambolled with buried treasure, bandanas, cutlasses and ear-rings.

We entered the Dickensian courtyard, the walls hung with old tin signs for petrol or railway posters. In the corner stood another fibreglass pirate with bare bosoms and a sign above her head – Captain Jacks. We entered a bare, gloomy hall like a school assembly room, with a bar at one end and some drinks machines around the side and more pictures of pirates and galleons. We went to the bar and the kindly waitress gave us some menus and showed us into another large room, set with some tables, where we saw the rest of the ride group, drinking and waiting for food.

We found a table and were soon joined by Mark and Charlie and shortly after by Richard and Emma – looking flushed and tired and damp from the shower – as we all were.

My phone still stubbornly refused to switch either on or off, but Ian managed to get a WIFI signal and googled what to do with a useless iPhone that won't work, and once I had the correct sequence of buttons to press and phrases to incant over the machine, success! As soon as my phone switched back on, I saw a message from my wife, asking whether I was back; I texted to let her know I was safe.

The food, when it eventually came, was surprisingly tasty and Ella – the waitress – was chatty and friendly. We told her we were doing LeJog.

'I did that,' she said.

'Really?' said Ian, not quite believing her.

'I walked it,' she said, 'virtually, during lockdown. There's an app. For my Granddad, raising money.'

She was young and slight, red-haired and eager with ringlets and tattoos and a bright, friendly face.

'Brilliant,' we all said in unison. 'Well done.'

Maybe our ride and we weren't so special, after all.

We walked back in the pitch darkness with a few wrong turnings and dead ends but made it eventually.

I didn't sleep well that night, as in fact I didn't any night, waking at about 1.30am, and then hourly intervals thereafter, until at 5.30am in the half-light I stirred and got out of bed.

I was sitting on the toilet looking at the Orbea, which was leaning against the wall, clearly visible from my perch. I couldn't tell if the front tyre was flat or just appeared to be so, as the wheel was sunk into the carpet. I got off the toilet and pressed the tyre – it was flat as a karaoke singer's voice. I couldn't believe it – another bloody puncture.

I removed the wheel and then sat on the bed and removed the tyre and then removed the tube. I took the tyre off the rim and examined every inch of it, running my finger around the inside looking for tell-tale puncture culprits. I found it eventually – a tiny sliver of glass embedded in the tyre. I prised it away and then cut off a piece of tyre boot and stuck that to the inside of the tyre, before re-installing the tyre on the rim and pumping it up as the sun rose meekly through the thin curtains.

I imagined the interview I would have when I reached John O'Groats:

'So, I'm here with Julian Hutchings, who's just completed LeJog, 900 miles across the length of Britain. Now Julian, can I call you Julian?'

'Er, yes, please do.'

'So, Julian, what is your abiding memory of LeJog?'

'Er, well punctures really, I suppose.'

'Punctures? Ah, but what about the challenge you put your body through? You really tested your body to the limit, didn't you? I bet you looked deep into your soul and found something that will set you up for the rest of your life.'

'No, punctures, actually.'

'Yes, but what about the glorious countryside you passed through? I bet you've seen bits of this country many of us can only dream about or see in a Michael Portillo or Sandi Toksvig programme.'

'No, still punctures.'

'Yes, but what about the friends you made? The camaraderie? Connections that will last for the rest of your days?'

'No, still punctures.'

'Well, thanks. Julian Hutchings everyone, what an achievement. If you're interested in doing LeJog and getting a load of punctures, then contact Julian.'

<u>Tavistock to Wookey Hole</u>

Miles: 101
Elevation: 6864ft
Ride time: 8h 10m
Average speed: 12.4mph

*

## Tuesday, 23 August 2021

## Wookey Hole, Somerset to Ludlow, Shropshire

One of the cyclists on our trip – Kevan – who had lost 4 stone for this trip and was raising money for a canine charity, was obviously not short of money. He had a Pinarello Dogma F12 with Dura-Ace Di2 electronic gears and wavy rimmed Zipp wheels that must have been 80mm deep. His bike was leaning against the van as I prepared to leave.

'Nice bike,' I said.

'Thanks, I needed a new bike for this trip, so I got this. I wanted an endurance bike.'

'What else do you have?' I said.

'A Cipollini, lovely bike, but too stiff, I can't ride it for more than about 50 miles.'

'What do you think of the ceramics?' I said, pointing to the over-size jockey wheels gracing the rear of his bike.

'The what?' he said.

'The jockey wheels,' I said, 'they're ceramic. Not cheap.'

'Dunno,' he said, 'never seen 'em before, the bike shop must have put them on.'

We left the odd hotel and the pirate restaurant of Wookey Hole, turned left, went about 200 metres and then straight into the toughest climb of the trip so far, and in fact probably the toughest climb of the whole trip. It was a narrow lane with high hedges, poorly surfaced but luckily very little traffic at that time of the morning. It started hard and got harder and then harder still, about half a mile long and gradients of 16, 17 and 18%.

Kevan came past me as I laboured up the climb, the tell-tale whirring of his electronic gears ringing in my ears as he changed down.

'Fucking hell,' he said, as he came past. 'It's a bastard.'

'Sure is,' I said, or probably thought I said, too out of breath to force any sound from my mouth.

Ian joined me at the top shortly after and we continued on a rolling, steady, straight-forward route, occasionally latching on to one of the other groups.

We were riding along a busy road heading toward Bristol when we came across Mark and Charlie, or Mac N Cheese as I was now calling them, who had stopped at the side of the road.

'What's up?' I said, as we rolled to a stop beside them.

'It's his cleat,' said Mark, pointing at Charlie, 'his cleat's broken.'

'There's a bus shelter a little further up,' said Ian, 'let's get off the road and see what we can do.'

We walked the 50 metres to the bus shelter where Ian and I both sat down in the shelter to have some snackage.

'It just broke,' said Charlie, pointing to his broken cleat.

'You shouldn't use road cleats,' said Ian, 'on a trip like this: mountain bike shoes and cleats are much better, you can walk on them.'

'That doesn't really help them now though, does it?' I said.

'Just saying,' said Ian, petulantly.

'We're trying to call Richard in the van,' said Mark, 'see if he's got any cleats on the van.'

'I'd get SPDs,' said Ian, still being unhelpful. 'Not much we can do really - good luck.'

We finished our snackage, saddled up like a couple of rustlers and headed off towards Clifton, leaving the father and son team stranded with a shoeless horse.

We soon reached Clifton, came down a short hairpin and were confronted with the famous suspension bridge, looking bright and shining in the morning sun. This delightful and spectacular bridge over the Avon gorge was designed by Brunel in 1835, I learned later while doing research for this book.

'Photo op,' said Ian, taking out his phone and recording some video for his family with the bridge as a backdrop.

There was a small coffee van parked called Chapter and Holmes just beside the start of the bridge and most of our group were sitting or standing around having coffee and snacks.

The coffee was delicious, the sun was warm, the benches comfortable and I ate a Tony chocolate bar while we paused to take in the view. Some of the stronger riders in the group had taken a detour to climb up Cheddar Gorge, which I was sorry to have missed, but resolved to return another day and climb it.

Traffic across the bridge was controlled by lights but being cyclists and thus knights of the road, we were able to cross at our leisure; there was a fabulous view to the side, looking down hundreds of feet to the valley, a trickle of water and the road snaking along far below.

The next few miles were largely flat and uneventful, until we travelled along a busy dual carriageway with trucks hurtling past us and finally, we reached the Severn Bridge and the gateway to Wales. There is a cycleway beside the road, and we paused at the start at the first of the giant suspension towers to look over the bridge to the vast expanse of the Severn, looking muddy, shallow and walkable far below. The wind blew strongly across the bridge and my GoPro was buffeted as we started to cross.

'Have you met the Severn bore?' I shouted to Ian, 'he'll tell you all about how this is one of the few tidal rivers in the world and the river rises many, many feet when the tide rolls in.'

'Up to 50 feet,' said Ian, who used to live in Chepstow on the Welsh side of the river, 'second highest in the world.'

'Are you sure you're not the Severn Bore?' I said.

But my elaborate and laboured joke was drowned in the sound of rushing cars and the wind whistling through the steel hawsers.

Once into Wales we rode through Chepstow without stopping, and then Monmouth, again without stopping, which Ian had I had visited (and stopped at) during our few days in Malvern a few weeks earlier, and then followed a beautiful gently rolling route through the Wye valley, the river glistening to our right until we reached Tintern Abbey for lunch.

Tintern Abbey was ruined, dark and forbidding despite the bright sunshine, and we searched for a café for some lunch.

We went to the café and pub which had a sign outside, 'PRE-BOOKED TABLES ONLY, NO SEATING.' Despite this rather unfriendly welcome, we queued inside for coffee and cold drinks, but the food options were decidedly limited, and we had to settle for carrot cake and a packet of crisps each.

It soon became apparent on this trip, that due to a combination of Brexit and Covid, many hospitality venues – hotel, restaurants, cafes, pubs – were desperately short of staff and either weren't open at all, or closed early, or had a limited menu. In fact, in at least two of the hotels we stayed at, we had to order our food two days in advance, which meant that the Ride Leaders came round with a short menu and a piece of paper and we had to write down what we wanted to eat two days hence, with some hilarious and bizarre consequences as people tried to remember what they had wanted to eat 48 hours earlier and whether they still wanted it now. We eventually reached Hereford, a busy unattractive town, with crowded roundabouts and impatient drivers, where Ian and I decided to stop in the shopping centre for more food.

There are two things that are uppermost in one's mind when doing LeJog and they are pedalling and food. Pedalling was and became automatic – one sat on the saddle and pedalled and tried not to think of the risk of saddle sores or one's aching arse and the saddle sores that were, at this very moment, hatching and expanding in the gaps and cracks between one's legs, in the sweaty, damp recesses of one's shorts.

Which left food – what to eat, when to eat, where to eat, how much to eat, would it be filling enough. One worried about bonking, not so much that one *would* bonk, but that one *might* bonk and of the clammy weakness and sugar craving that accompanied bonking. Most days we stopped 3 and often 4 times at cafes or restaurants, and often also at junctions or other convenient places to chew on a cereal bar or squeeze a gel.

In the ride details which Bike Adventures had sent out before the trip started, they had advised against bringing large quantities of energy bars, on the basis that it added unnecessary weight and there were plenty of bike shops and food shops that we would pass while cycling. I had brought a few Veloforte energy bars, and I had brought energy gels - Kendal Mint ones which had a pleasant minty (surprisingly) taste and some produced by Veloforte, including an espresso coffee one which provided a tasty shot of caffeine. I carried one of each every day and always had them – they provided a much-needed energy boost, particularly towards the end of the ride.

However, it was important to try and eat proper hot food – Ian developed a craving for soup, easily digestible calories and always accompanied by bread and on several occasions, I joined him. Cakes and pastries were all well and good for the mid-morning snack, but at lunchtime we wanted to eat proper food – bread, sandwiches, pasta, chips, rice – although pasta, a dish of plain penne with olive oil and butter, often wanted, often craved, was never actually an option.

The last leg from Hereford to Ludlow was tiring – it was a poorly surfaced road, rolling although not with any very hard climbs, but maybe we were tired on this, our third day of riding. We finally reached Ludlow and thought our troubles were over, but the route took us on a sharp, final, steep climb, not long but a final sting in the tail before we reached the Travelodge and our perch for the night. It sat on an industrial estate with a large Tesco, a petrol station a giant pet emporium and various other DIY stores.

The Travelodge itself didn't have a restaurant but there was one next door, the usual Harvester type menu – chips with everything and a nod to ethnic cuisine – Mexican, an Indian dish, Korean chicken wings, a hardly Italian lasagne.
I ordered cheesy nachos.

'Be careful,' the waitress (or 'server', as we must learn to call her) said, 'they're hot.'

But they weren't. Bits of the melted cheese had maybe dated the odd bit of heat, but the nachos were cold, stubbornly not crisp and as I delved deeper into the tepid bowl the whole disintegrated into a cold, beige, chilly mess. But it was calories, I suppose.

I followed that with a lamb and mint burger with chips and coleslaw - calories again, which was pleasant enough, although the burger had an odd, antiseptic, Savlony taste as if the chef, or cook, had a sore finger and had dipped his or her Savlon coated digit in the mince. For dessert, on one of the few occasions on this trip, I had a berry citrus sundae, a vast concoction of ice cream, berries, some lemon peel, buckets of cream on top and finally a sort of lemon drizzle or spittle on top.

I slept poorly again, regularly awakened by the sound of lorries rushing by on the main road near-by.

Wookey Hole to Ludlow

Mileage: 103.5
Elevation: 7211ft
Ride time: 7h50m
Average speed: 13.2mph

*

## Wednesday, 24 August 2021

## Ludlow, Shropshire to Chorley, Lancashire

The fourth day in and a pattern was firmly established.

Get up
Eat
Ride bike
Eat
Ride bike
Eat
Ride bike
Eat
Ride bike (a bit more)
Put clothes on to wash
Put electronics on to charge
Check Strava
Shower
Eat
Sleep
Get up
And so on

The night before, Richard had asked if the restaurant could serve breakfast before 7.30 so we could make an early start on what was to be the longest day of riding.

'7.15,' the server had said.

'7?' said Richard.

'7.15,' she said.

We all gathered outside the restaurant at 7.10, a dry and clear day but still cool on that Welsh morning. Staff drove up in their cars and disappeared inside and at 7.15 we tried the door which stayed firmly bolted.

The riders, some in their lycra, some still in civilian clothes, all wiping sleep from their eyes and rubbing or stretching tired legs, stood in small groups and tutted.

Time slipped past slowly like a bad man creeping down an alley in the dark.

7.20 and the door was tried again, and again at 7.25 and again at 7.26, 7.27, 7.28 and 7.29. At 7.30 the door was carefully unbolted, and we all trooped inside.

'I thought it was 7.15?' said Ian.

'Let it go mate,' I said.

We set off at 8.15, easing gradually into the ride, trying to uncoil our aching limbs.

My daughter, Rachel, was a strong advocate of yoga and the benefits of stretching before and after a ride and had taught me a few key moves and poses. I set out with good intentions – planning to stretch after every ride and stretch again in the mornings. I also brought along a plastic roller, a bit like a rounders bat or very large dildo, planning to roll it un my thighs and calves every evening. In the end, I did a few desultory stretches after some rides but never before any, and used the roller a few times, but without much effort or enthusiasm. Maybe I was just lucky, but my legs stayed relatively pain-free.

Ian and a few of the other guys had brought along massage guns, a sort of combination electric hammer drill and vibrator, and used this on their aching limbs, although the sound must have caused some consternation in adjoining rooms, especially as some of the hotels we stayed in had walls as thin as rice paper.

'Does it work,' I asked.

'Yep,' said Ian and I resolved to get one, and not use it either.

I'm beginning to lose track of time. I was cycling along today, and I couldn't work out what day it was. Partly, I'm tired and a bit disoriented, partly it's because I haven't had the TV or radio on since Friday and so have no reference points and partly it's because I have no real need to know what day it is – we're on our way to John O'Groats and eventually we will get there, but the day and the date doesn't seem so important.

It's as if we're in a bubble – a moving bubble of broken tarmac and shit roads, of tyres and chains and handlebar tape, drinks bottles that taste of damp plastic, of energy gels, carrot cake, endless lattes and the odd bag of crisps, rubbish drivers and punctured tyres. Although the last seems to have stopped, for now. It's like my body has shut down, to focus on the essentials of turning the pedals, breathing, pumping blood to the legs, sweating and an endless stream of liquid dripping from my nose. What is it about cycling that makes one's nose drip?

'Charlie Watts has died,' I said to Ian, as we rode along. 'Sad.'

He gave me a sideways look.

'That was yesterday,' he said.

'Oh.'

'Cycling is like life,' I said, a bit later.

'How's that?' he said.

'You just have to keep pedalling,' I said. 'We will make it to John O'Groats, we just have to keep pedalling. Might be tired, might be hungry, might be feeling knackered with aching limbs and tight calves but if we keep pedalling, we will get there. Can't miss. Wait and see.'

'Shut up and pedal,' said Ian, which was my advice, turned back on me.

Ian lived in Newport, not far from Ludlow and knew these roads and was not happy with the route we were on.

'This is ridiculous,' he said, as we rolled along through the not unattractive, but hardly inspiring Shropshire countryside. 'I can't believe they're sending us on this route – it's miles out of our way, adding unnecessary hills, stupid! I'm going to speak to someone.'

'Let it go,' I said, 'enjoy the ride.'

'I can't.'

As we headed up one of Ian's unnecessary climbs, we came across Nick, a young lad who was on the trip and had seemed on the first few days like a fast racing snake so I was surprised that us two old duffers had caught him.

'You okay mate?' I said, as I drew alongside him.

'No,' he said, 'been up all night, puking, didn't sleep much. Think it was the scampi.'

'Word of advice, mate,' I said, unhelpfully, 'don't eat seafood on a trip like this.'

Poor Nick - laid low in Ludlow. I let him go, not wishing to get too close to any projectile vomiting that might be coming my way.

We carried on, through the village of Diddlebury, where I spent so long trying to think of a clever pun that by the time I had thought of it, we were through the village and out the other side and I'd forgotten it.

We arrived in Shrewsbury, Ian still huffing and tutting, and saw the van.

'There's no cafes on the route,' said Martin.

'I know somewhere,' said Ian, 'I know Shrewsbury.'

We continued, going off piste, my Wahoo furiously beeping and trying to re-route us back to the correct road.

A few hundred yards further on, near to Shrewsbury Abbey, we stopped at a café. When I had stopped at the bike shop in Crediton to buy an inner tube, I had also bought a couple of flapjacks made by Torq and I ate a Bakewell tart flavoured one as we sat outside the café drinking a coffee; it was delicious.

'Shrewsbury School is in Shrewsbury,' said Ian, a propos of nothing.

'No shit,' I said.

'Alma mater of Willie Rushton, Michael Palin and…er…' said Ian, 'some other people.'

'Wow,' I said, as I couldn't think of anything else to say.

We left Shrewsbury and passed through the oddly named town of Wem and then Whitchurch some 25 miles further on where we went looking for a place to eat lunch. There was a dearth of suitable looking places, but we found the Café Bon Sol near the centre of town and settled down outside.

The waitress, whose name we learned subsequently was Jasmine, came to take our order and I ordered a coronation chicken sandwich.

'What sort of bread do you have?' I asked, thinking I'd be offered sourdough, granary, baguette, panini or any of the other continental flavoured options so familiar to us poncey southerners.

Jasmine looked at me oddly.

'White or brown,' she said. I settled for white.

Ian wanted a cheese and onion sandwich and a bowl of soup but for some reason – maybe he was distracted thinking of the limited bread options - asked for a toasted bacon and onion sandwich.

A different waitress brought out the food, including an untoasted sandwich for Ian.

'I asked for it toasted,' he said, sending it back.

'Doesn't look much like cheese,' he said to me.

'You didn't order cheese,' I said, 'you ordered bacon, I was wondering why.'

'I'm tired,' said Ian.

My coronation chicken sandwich was an odd pink in colour as if they had put the chicken in a bowl and mixed it with some salad cream and a bit of ketchup, and it had the same vaguely antiseptic taste that I had encountered previously – not unpleasant but there was no hint of the curry flavour I had come to expect from that dish.

The waitress brought Ian's sandwich back, but a newly toasted, tired, bacon and raw onion sandwich did not tickle his palate; however, he seemed to enjoy the soup.

After leaving Whitchurch, we continued onto Nantwich where we saw the van and the sun came out and where we were later joined by Mark and Charlie. Mark was struggling with his phone which was running out of charge. I had lent Charlie my power bank when we left Ludlow, but this didn't seem to work for him either.

'It keeps on losing charge,' he said.

'You boys don't have a lot of luck, do you?' I said, helpfully.

I offered to lend them my spare Wahoo, but they seemed oddly reluctant, preferring to soldier on with their own useless gadgets rather than accept the generosity of (sort of) strangers.

Out of Nantwich and we rolled through some attractive, largely flat Cheshire countryside, passing many large mansions set back from the road.

'This is Posh and Becks territory,' said Ian.

'I thought they lived in Hertfordshire,' I said.

'When he was at Manchester,' said Ian, 'not now.'

We finally arrived at a big roundabout with many exits, and I had trouble seeing our route on the Wahoo. The Wahoo had a re-routing function if you went off course, which could be quite useful, but it happened almost instantaneously and instead of saying, 'turn round, you should have gone left,' which was what you wanted, it sent you off on a different route which might involve riding to the next roundabout and turning round. After this happened several times, leaving us circum-navigating a busy roundabout for the umpteenth time, I got fed up and said to Ian we should head to a KFC and look at the map.

'Good idea,' said Ian, who was hungry again. 'What do you want?'

'Milkshake,' I said, 'strawberry, preferably, chocolate otherwise.'

'Milkshake is off,' said Ian, 'Brexit, or Covid, or one of them, or both; anyway, off.'

Why milkshakes were off, I never discovered. 'I'll have Lipton iced tea then.'

While Ian was ordering a Zinger burger and the drinks at the counter, I looked at the yellow route sheets we had been given. On the first day the Ride Leaders had handed out a big bundle of yellow printed route sheets, which showed the route in meticulous detail, with various mysterious abbreviations suggesting TL (turn left) or TL (turn right) or other ones which I did not understand. Each day I had extracted the sheets for that day's ride and put them in a plastic folder in my back pocket in case they should be needed. As I never looked at them, I had resolved that morning to stop carrying them but decided that Wednesday would be the last day. Now, with the help of a very helpful chap in the KFC and careful study of the yellow sheets, I was able to identify the roundabout we were stalled at and the correct exit to take, while drinking my iced tea and Ian chomped his chips and ploughed through his burger.

Newly energised and with our directions sorted we pressed on over the Warburton toll bridge. This bridge was built in 1890 and spans the Manchester Ship Canal. The toll - 12p for cars, cyclists go free – was set in 1890 and curiously and interestingly, has never been increased.

We then continued through Warrington – a hard, depressed, tired and hungry looking town with many houses that looked like they were worth less than our bikes and then another 20 miles or so including some climbs – not hard but we were both flagging a bit, having ridden over 100 miles, until we finally rolled into Chorley and the welcome sight of a nice-looking Premier Inn.

'Surely it's Chorley,' I said.

Ian was tired and did not laugh.

'I can't be bothered going to dinner,' he texted, when we had reached our rooms. 'I'm getting a Chinese via Deliveroo.'

I went to the restaurant and met Nick, a barrister who was waiting outside, having also arrived later than the others who had already gone in, so I ended up having dinner with him.

The food was pleasant, and I ordered some very tasty, as they proved to be, crispy Korean glazed chicken wings, and then a beef lasagne, which I had been looking forward to but proved to be stodgy and dense like damp newspaper that someone had trodden brown grit into. And chips – which I scoffed. And a gin and tonic. And lots of water.

Ludlow to Chorley

Miles: 117
Elevation: 5282ft

Ride time: 8h 22m
Average speed: 14mph

*

## Thursday 25 August 2021

## Chorley, Lancashire to Carlisle, Cumbria

Breakfast the next morning proved to be the best of the trip. A groaning buffet with a wide choice - freshly made eggs - scrambled, fried, poached or boiled - bacon, sausages (properly cooked, as they often weren't on this trip), black pudding and all the other ingredients of a proper full English, which I didn't really want and never ate when at home, but it always seemed the thing to do when one was on holiday, which this was, even if it didn't always feel like it. The coffee was hot and plentiful, the juices were cold and fresh and there were different types of bread – not just white and brown – and there were staff on duty – a rarity in many of the establishments we visited. I ate 2 pain au chocolat, a croissant, a toasted crumpet with butter and Nutella, which I had not eaten for years and brought back many happy memories, as well as a yoghurt, coffee, orange juice, two sausages, bacon (quite hard, it often is, doesn't keep well), fried and scrambled eggs and two hash browns; I felt ready for the day.

The Premier Inn breakfast room had opened at 7am so we had the chance of an earlier start. Today, we were heading to Carlisle, getting ever closer to Scotland and our final destination at that fingertip of land.

Outside, we saw Nick who was struggling with his bike.

'What's up?' I said.

'I came off yesterday, up that final climb, and bent the rear mech.'

'Risky,' said Martin, putting the bike up on a stand. 'If we try and bend it back, it might break.'

'Silly question,' I said, 'have you got a spare mech on the van?'

'No,' he said, 'there's too many different designs – every bike has their own.'

Which does one make one wonder why this couldn't be standardised across the bike industry, along with through axle design and sizes and bottom brackets – it would make life easier for everyone.

'Maybe if I just don't use the lowest gears,' said Nick, 'what do you think?

'Risky,' said Martin, 'if the mech shifts too far it will go into the rear wheel and then you'll really have problems. Maybe it's safer not to ride it.'

'Not ride it?' said Nick, indignant, 'I'm doing the bloody LeJog; of course I'm going to ride it.'

'Be careful,' said Martin.

'Sod it,' said Nick and set off, gingerly.

Ian and I set off at a fast pace, legs feeling fine, a cloudy day but the temperature just right – not too hot, not too cold – as most days had been. After 30 miles, we reached Lancaster, passing various little pelotons on the way, me on the front, head down, taking little notice of the scenery but fair tonking.

'Coffee,' I think,' said Ian. 'Snackage.'

Lancaster seemed like an attractive town, and we veered off the breadcrumb route into the centre to find a café. It was very pleasant, affluent and continental – cobbled streets, little squares, fine Georgian houses, pavement tables, the aroma of fresh brewed coffee and pastries softly filling the air.

I went inside to view the cake offerings while Ian phoned his wife and then we settled down at a pavement table. I was in the mood for a teacake with plenty of butter and jam, but they didn't do tea-cakes - too prosaic, too basic, too not continental enough.

The waitress brought our coffees on a little wooden tray with a small glass of water – intricate patterns traced on the frothy surface by a skilful barista. On the tray, placed designer-like midway between the coffee and the water was a small cube of pink wafer, like a building block for a child's construction set, which soon disappeared. And food – two items for me, a berry Bakewell tart and a home-made flapjack (flapjacks are always home-made), dense with oats and fruit and grains, to make up for all the pacing I had been doing.

We left the café and headed back to the route and there ran into a 6-rider peloton from our group, which we latched onto. Out through Lancaster, over the very attractive Lune suspension bridge, built to commemorate the Millennium in 2000, and then pushing on towards the Lake District.

After some 47 miles, Harry, who was leading the peloton, pulled to a halt by a small stone bridge over a pretty stream.

'It's half-way,' he said, 'photo stop.'

We all lined up on the bridge and flagged down a passing cyclist who took our group photo – all with our thumbs up - as the campervans and caravans, motorhomes and motorbikes thundered past on their staycation route to the Lakes.

So far on the trip my bike had carried: a saddlebag containing 2 tubes, tyre levers, $CO_2$ canister and a multi-tool; a top tube bag which contained my GoPro on a mouth mount, so I could remove it while riding, stick it in my mouth like a boxer's mouth-guard and chomp down on it while filming; and a front handlebar bag which contained a rain jacket, my snackage, a small lock, a front light, a spare rear light, another $CO_2$ canister and another tube – I wasn't taking any risks.

Today, I had decided that I was putting stuff in the bar-bag because it was there and not because it was essential, and had left the bag behind, instead putting the rain jacket and a few other items in my jersey pockets instead. However, I wasn't happy with the weight and the bulk lying on my back, so when we saw the van shortly after, I retrieved my bar-bag, emptied my groaning pockets and put it back on the bike.

The sun had come out and it was getting distinctly hot, so we all paused at the van for more water and more sunscreen.

Ian was a firm believer in the efficacious benefits of chamois cream and half the weight of his luggage was taken up with multiple pots of Assos cream. Every time we stopped for a meal break, or a toilet stop, Ian would disappear into the toilet or behind a bush (depending on the location) and rummage in his shorts with a handful of soothing cream. Today was no exception, so as the rest of us filled up on water, Ian was to be found, half-hidden by the door of the van, fumbling around in his shorts with a large tube of cream gripped in his fist.

'What you should do,' I said, having observed this ritual rather more times than I felt was strictly necessary, 'is have a tube of cream gripped between your legs at the top of your thighs and every time you pedal it could squeeze out a set amount of cream, a bit like an injection engine. I might design something when I get back.'

'You do that,' he said, wiping his greasy hands on some kitchen roll, 'I'd buy it.'

On we rode, over rolling pleasant roads (except for the motorhomes) in the warm, now hot sunshine until we reached the tourist trap of Kendal.

'Lunch,' said Ian, no doubt sensing the opportunity for more chamois cream delving.

We found a nice-looking tearoom on the main street and entered a small courtyard, set with a few rickety metal tables. As we lent our bikes against the wall, we were joined by Nick, he of the fall and the damaged rear mech.

'How's the bike?' I said.

'Brilliant,' he said, 'I found this amazing mechanic in a village, just some guy in his garage fixing bikes, but he sorted the mech, adjusted the gears and it's better than it ever was. Absolutely amazing.'

'How much?' I asked, always interested in the minutiae of commerce.

'Well,' he said, 'I asked him how much and he said £10.' I said, "I'm not giving you that, I'll give you £20, plus I'll give £20 to charity, plus I'll share your name all over social media, so you get more business."'

'Nice, although he probably would have preferred the £40,' I said, always interested in commerce.

'What's his name?'[13]

'Don't remember,' said Nick. 'What're you eating?'

We sat for some time in that bright sunshine, Ian and Nick both with their heads swathed in Johnny Depp bandanas against the heat and consumed a hearty lunch – a tuna mayonnaise sandwich for me, pleasant although rather heavier on bread than tuna, while Ian and Nick both tucked into soup and jacket potatoes. I've never been a big fan of jacket potatoes – which is a shame as they are a very good energy source while cycling.

My friend Simon, who knows about these things, had tried to teach me some basic nutrition, including the difference between low GI and high GI foods, and the differences between proteins and carbohydrate and their impact on weight, but it mostly went over my head. However, one of the advantages of this trip, was that Simon's strictures against eating what I liked was flung out the window – defenestrated, you could say.

Leaving Kendal, we soon approached the iconic, the marquee, the piece de resistance climb of the whole trip, lauded in all the end-to end records, and the scene of Les Roberts, my fellow Old

---

[13] Rock Garden Cycles, The Garage, Marsh Bank Works, CW5 5HH, www.rockgardencycles.co.uk Tel: 07891 491835

Portlian, being blown off his bike in driving winds and rain, during their 2007 assault on LeJog – Shap Fell.

'Shap Fell,' said Ian, sagely, as we paused at a little side road for more chamois action.

'I remember,' he went on, like an Icelandic story-teller, 'back in 2007 when I rode this – driving rain it was, and cold wind, thunder and lightning, hail, and snow. Horrible.'

For us this time, however, the weather Gods shone, despite a strong head wind, and in addition the road was smooth and newly re-surfaced and surprisingly quiet, without the endless streams of caravan traffic and elderly men on motorbikes we had expected. Although a long climb of some 5 miles or so, the gradient was benign, never reaching above 10% and mostly significantly lower than that; all in all, I felt that I had done longer climbs and I had done steeper climbs, and indeed both longer and steeper climbs.

I probably could have done it in the big ring and crowed about the feat for years to come as I bored my grand-kids with how their grand-dad had conquered the fearsome Shap Fell in the big ring back in that bleak mid-Covid, post-Brexit summer of 2021, before the world changed. But I didn't. I moved into the small ring and pedalled steadily towards the top, or near the top for the famous lay-by - scene of so many iconic photos of end-to-enders slumped over their bikes in the fog and the murky half-light – is in fact just below the 'summit' – although summit gives it more gravitas than it perhaps deserves, as the road gradually flattens and then is flat, before it starts to descend.

There appeared to be some sort of cairn or monument on the south side of the road, probably marking the top, although I didn't get close enough to check; but here, on the northern approach, there was nothing to commemorate our great achievement. Ian soon joined Nick (who had set off before us) and I and we took our inevitable photos before starting the descent.

Although I was stronger and quicker on the climbs than Ian, when the road turned downhill the situation was reversed – being 6'4" and significantly heavier than me, he could develop a fearsome momentum, like a bowling ball on a slide, and it did not take long before I heard the swish of his wheels and he eased past me on the steady downhill run which took us all the way to Penrith.

More fuel was called for in Penrith, but we struggled to find a café. Eventually, we found a pub with outdoor seating in the centre of town, where we found Mark and Charlie, who had left Kendal before us – they must have done, how else to explain their arrival first?

The sun was still shining, and it was still warm in this late afternoon and the seats were filled with various Penrith waifs and strays who all seemed to be getting steadily and determinedly drunk. There was little actual food on offer, so we settled for cold drinks, coffee, crisps and bags of nuts and the kindly barmaid offered to fill our water bottles.

Ian and I left Mark and Charlie still warming their seats and we headed off for the final 20 miles or so to Carlisle, which proved to be on an almost completely straight, slightly undulating quiet road, very pleasant to ride but also tiring with no opportunity to freewheel as we were constantly pedalling; nonetheless we managed a steady 17mph average.

'It's like life,' I said to Ian again, at one point, 'you just have to keep pedalling.'

'Shut up and keep pedalling,' said Ian, who had heard my cod philosophy before and had no time for it.

We entered Carlisle, which appeared a busy town of no obvious beauty (although we may well have missed the beauty) and had some difficulty finding the Ibis Hotel – our home for the night. The Wahoo beeped on the main street and said we had arrived, but in our tired and disorientated state (common during these 9 days) we could not immediately see it. We turned down a side street and accosted various locals and eventually retraced our steps and found it, its doorway not obvious and sandwiched between a Chinese 'all you can eat buffet' restaurant and a city gym.

I squeezed my bike into the lift and found my room on the second floor - a small box with a window overlooking the carpark, and a small box for a bathroom with an annoying step up, which I managed to trip on every time I went in.

Still, we had arrived at about 6.15, one of the earliest finishes of the trip so far. At the briefing before we left Penzance, Mike had said there was no real point in rushing from one stop to the next, as, due to Covid, most places did not allow entry to the rooms until at least 4pm, and in Scotland we might be lucky to be allowed in before 6pm.

The Ibis, being a (very) low budget option, did not have a restaurant, so evening meals were left up to us. Some of the group fancied the 'all you can eat' Chinese Buffet and disappeared in there, but I was not a fan of Chinese food and still had a hankering for some pasta.

Ian, Nick and I set out on a restaurant hunt, and were joined by Richard and Martin, the two Ride Leaders. We found a couple of nice-looking pizza places, but they were both full, until one offered a table for two, so Richard and Martin took that, and the three of us set off looking for something else. Eventually we found a rather posh looking hotel which offered us a table in the bar area and a decent menu. There was very loud music playing, not what we wanted after a long, hot, tiring ride. 'Any chance of turning the music down?' Ian asked the waiter when he arrived to take our drinks order.

'Not really,' said the waiter, 'it's the bar area, the customers like it.'

'I'm a customer, too,' said Ian after he'd gone, or possibly while he was still there.

'Let it go mate,' I said.

'Can we have another table in the restaurant?' Ian asked, when the waiter returned.

'Um, well you could,' said the waiter, 'but there's a wedding party in there, so you might find it even noisier.'

So we stayed where we were and suffered the banging music and the wedding party shouts and banter throughout the meal.

But the food was very good, although the service was a bit odd.

Nick ordered a lime juice and sparkling water, and I said I'd have the same plus a gin and tonic. Nick then received a glass of blackcurrant juice, which he was happy to drink, while I got my gin and tonic, but no lime juice and sparkling water. It seemed surprising that such a simple order – Ian had ordered a beer – could go so spectacularly wrong.

I ate a pea, asparagus and parmesan soup (having developed a taste for soup, following Ian's lead), which was very tasty although only tepid, and then a beefburger with triple cooked chips and a side order of sourdough with dipping oil - sourdough clearly having reached these parts despite bypassing Whitchurch. The burger was tasty, but the chips were distinctly pale and anaemic, perhaps they were only double and not triple cooked, but I stocked up on the sourdough for my carb hit.

Nick was a big rugger and cricket fan, as was Ian, who had spent much of the trip checking the test match scores on his phone and announcing them to me in an occasionally triumphant voice.

'Root's on 42,' he would shout, as he swept past me on a downhill section.

'India, 81 for 1,' he would shout, far behind me on a climb, his words almost lost in the head wind.

With a fellow afficionado, he was in his element, and they found much to bore each other with, so I found myself gradually zoning out of the conversation and concentrating on eating and drinking, which proved a pleasant way to spend the evening.

I spent another restless night; this being main street Carlisle, lined with pubs and clubs and various other dens of iniquity, there was much noise in the night, including some distinct banging and crashing at about 4am which may have been furniture, or even people, being thrown through windows. That's Northern entertainment, I suppose.

## Chorley to Carlisle

Miles: 99.3
Elevation: 5030ft
Ride time: 7h 03m
Average speed: 14.1

*

## Friday 26 August 2021

## Carlisle, Cumbria to Kilsyth, Scotland

Today, we cross the border into bonnie Scotland!

Ian was on the front (for a change) and set a furious pace for the 10 miles or so to Gretna Green and the Scottish border. Although not the first to leave, we swept past all comers on the road, and reached Scotland afore ye.

We paused at the 'Scotland Welcomes You' sign for photos before soon setting off again. The route then took us through fine Scottish countryside with Scottish trees, Scottish fields, Scottish sheep, Scottish hedges and pitted and poor Scottish roads, all of which looked distinctly like the English variants that we had been riding through up to now. Soon we reached Lockerbie, scene of that appalling terrorist attack on the Pan-Am plane on 21 December 1988 in which 270 people including 11 residents of Lockerbie had been murdered, although we did not see, or go looking for, the memorial which must be there.

We stopped at a café in Lockerbie and found the biggest contrast with England we had encountered so far, and that was to do with the attitude to Covid.

The Scots were very hot on Covid; the rules were quite clear, NO MASK NO ENTRY, and each establishment required a test and trace form to be filled out or an app to be scanned, and the rules were rigidly enforced, both by proprietors and by peer group pressure. The contrast with England could not have been more marked – in England one had the impression no-one gave a shit, either about test and trace or about mask wearing, but here in Scotland people cared.

'You get the feeling,' I said to Ian, as we sat eating our enormous teacakes with butter and jam, 'that in Scotland the Government cares about trying to keep the population safe, but in England they couldn't care less.'

'As with many other things,' said Ian.

While we were eating, a message came through on the WhatsApp saying that the van had been delayed. Shortly thereafter, Mark arrived, sans his son, and informed us that poor Charlie's pedal had fallen off and that he was in the van heading for Dumfries and searching for a bike shop, which sounded like the start of a short story. That pair did not seem to have much luck.

'Or,' I said to Ian, when Mark was out of ear-shot, 'maybe some better checks on their kit and equipment and a bit more planning wouldn't have gone amiss.'

'I don't think they're gonna make it,' said Ian, like a soothsayer declaiming a dark prophesy.

'Why do you say that?' I said.

'Mark my words,' he said, mysteriously.

'I don't agree,' I said. 'Mark's strong and Charlie's young and they seem pretty determined, if their kit holds up.'

We left Mark behind to source his own teacake and set off through the attractive border country for the next town, which was called Moffat, whose main street was full of parked cars. As we rode through, we saw some of the group siting outside a café called the Rumbling Tum, so we stopped for food.

Again, the Covid rules were being rigidly enforced – despite tables being set up outside, there was a chain across the entrance, and we had to wait, masked up, until a waiter came out and seated us at a safe distance from the other diners.

I studied the menu.

'Scotch Pie,' said Ian suddenly, with a gleam of triumph in his eye, 'that's what I'm having. Have that.'

'What is it?' I said.

'Scotch pie,' he said, 'like a pasty, we used to have it at football matches.' Ian was Scottish by birth and liked to extol the virtues of the old country at every suitable opportunity, and many unsuitable ones.

The pie came; it was the size of a small pork pie, and looked like a suet pudding, a rather unappetising undercooked beige colour, with a paltry filling that may have been engaged to some indeterminate meat at some point in its life but had probably been jilted at the altar. However, it was heavily dowsed in pepper, whether to disguise or impart some flavour was hard to judge, but it added a not unpleasant spiciness to it, and I ended up wolfing it down. Maybe it *was* wolf.

Leaving Moffat, and after Ian had visited the van for more chamois cream, it having arrived and deposited Charlie with new pedals, we soon hit another climb, another long one of 4 miles or so, but of fairly gentle average gradient, rising through bare, green rolling hills; but it was a fine road, smooth and newish, and with little traffic.

Inevitably, the shallow climb was followed by a shallow descent following the course of the River Tweed. Although shallow, it was a very long one, meaning that I could freewheel for a short amount of time, but usually had to pedal, although the road surface was not quite so new and not quite so good. The last mile of the descent into the village of Broughton was dreadful, as if they had run out of money – pitted and rutted with crumbling tarmac - which made cycling very slow and also quite dangerous.

'Why don't you pay your fucking council tax and get your roads fixed,' Ian shouted after each passing car, startling a middle-aged, elegantly dressed lady who was walking her dog.

'Let it go mate,' I said.

'I can't,' he said.

'Fuck!' I shouted, as I hit another tree root or massive pothole, bump, bump, bumping along like Christopher Robin going downstairs and was almost thrown from my bike, 'fucking hell, these roads are shit.'

The roads, incidentally, and this was another thing one learned on LeJog, are equally as bad in each county of England; and in Scotland, despite their hard work over Covid (not that the two things are connected), they were no better.

'I've ridden on cobbles in Flanders that are better than these,' I said to Ian at one point.

One sometimes had the feeling that the last people to work on the roads of Britain with any degree of success or effort, were the Romans.

Turning left in Broughton, we finally reached a much nicer road, with a steady climb that took us up to the town of Biggar. Halfway up the climb, I received a torrent of abuse from a motorcyclist who obviously wasn't happy that I was trying to avoid the shit and stones at the side of the road and was instead riding a safe distance from the kerb. Abuse from other road users is an occupational hazard as all cyclists will know, but one does wish that they have a nasty, and preferably fatal, accident as punishment.

Biggar was a substantial town, bigger than Broughton which was smaller than Biggar, and we found a café on the main street, where we met up with Nick and then Mark and Charlie, who arrived shortly after, Charlie now safely pedalling on new pedals. We found a table on the pavement, and I went to order. Both Ian and I spotted macaroni cheese on the menu and, craving pasta every day and not finding it, we thought our luck was in.

As a result of Covid, one had to order at a little hatch, like the hatch into a prisoner's cell, so I went and queued and placed the order. After about 10 minutes during which we got more and more hungry in anticipation, a lady leaned out of the hatch and shouted that macaroni cheese was finished and we had to choose something else. Ian was hungry and ordered a jacket potato with haggis and the inevitable soup, while I chose the coronation chicken sandwich.

This, when it came, and there was a substantial wait, proved to be very tasty and was reassuringly yellow, as opposed to pink, and actually tasted of chicken and curry, as opposed to the antiseptic taste I was becoming used to and, truth be told, rather enjoyed.

Leaving Biggar, Ian and I, Mark and Charlie and Richard and Emma (who had joined us), formed a little peloton which we stuck with for several miles, until Richard and Emma drifted off the back and the remaining four of us continued all the way to

Kilsyth, which is halfway between, and a bit to the north, of Glasgow and Edinburgh.

As Ian and I were riding along, we kept on being passed by a Mazda Bongo campervan with a couple of bikes on the back. We would cycle on and see it parked at the side of the road, with the driver pretending to look at the map, so we would pass it, and shortly after it would pass us again and then a bit later, we would see it parked by the side of the road again.

'Do you see that?' I said to Ian.

'What?'

'That van.'

'What van?'

'That van, that Mazda Bongo, that campervan! Haven't you seen it?'

'Oh, that, what about it?'

'Christ, this is hard work,' I said, 'I think it's stalking us. Like in Easy Rider. I'll be Peter Fonda.'

'Let it go,' said Ian.

We passed through some rather tired looking conurbations and then out onto a glorious rolling route, with a couple of short, sharp climbs, down a fabulous descent, through a winding wooded area, past a small lake shimmering in the late light, the sun still shining, the sky a deep blue with nary a cloud, some of the finest cycling of the trip and the hottest day we had so far experienced.

At one point we passed through a small village, and I was first to the top of the climb and stopped and waited for the others. As I sat on my bike at the side of the road, a little old lady, who was watering her plants on the other side of the road, said good evening, so I said good evening and commented on what a lovely evening it was.

'Aye,' she said, 'would you like some cool water?'

'That's very kind of you,' I said, 'but I'm fine.'

'Where have you come from?' she asked.

'Carlisle,' I said.

'Och, she said, 'Carlisle, such a long way.'

'And before that, Land's End. We're going to John O'Groats.'

'Och,' she said, 'and in such hot weather too. You picked a lovely day for it.'

'That we have,' I said, 'that we have.'

At that point, Emma, who had joined our peloton with Richard, came toiling up the hill.

The lady saw her and said, 'och, and ye've got a wee girlie with you.'

What a sweet lady she was, if a bit patronising to Emma.

We finally reached the hotel in Kilsyth, after a laborious detour down some cycle routes, over bridges, across roundabouts, through tunnels, which I was convinced were taking us round in circles, and then found the hotel – a converted boathouse by an attractive marina in a canal basin.

As on many of the nights, perhaps due to Covid, the group was split between two hotels, but Ian and I were booked into this one and it seemed very nice, and certainly a pleasant change from the glorified multi storey car park which had been the Ibis in Carlisle.

Ian and I, masked up, went inside to the reception which was part of the busy bar and restaurant area.

'We've come to check in,' said Ian, sweaty and tired, with chamois cream leaking from his shorts.

'Take a seat,' said the girl behind the bar, 'we're busy.'

'Fucking hell,' said Ian, who was not impressed, sotto voce to me.

Shortly thereafter, the manager, or deputy manager came over.

'Evening gentlemen,' he said. 'You're the last to check in, just looking for the keys.'

Ian and I stood and waited, 112 miles in our legs and desperate for a shower.

'I can't seem to find the keys,' said the manager or deputy manager. He made a phone call to the manager or the deputy manager for key advice.

'Come with me,' he said to us, eventually. 'I think I've found them.'

We finally gained entry to the rooms, which proved very pleasant - spacious and well-equipped with a view over the boats in the marina, the hills beyond, and the sun gradually setting over the water.

After the usual nightly ritual – washing clothes, showering, charging electronics, I headed out of the room to the restaurant and met Ian just coming out of his room. There, ahead of us, in the car park, silent and deadly like an assassin, and firmly locked up, was the Mazda Bongo.
'We're done for,' I said to Ian, 'he's tracked us down. What should we do?'

'Keep calm, 'said Ian, 'act normal.'

'I can't,' I said, 'I'm nervous.'

'Try.'

We entered the very pleasant restaurant and found a table, where Roy, Steve and Mike were already seated. The food was very tasty – I had an apple, walnut and blue cheese salad to start, my body craving some vegetables and fruit to stave off scurvy after the endless diet of chips and carbs, cakes and sugar; and then had a pizza which was okay, but is never quite as nice as you want it to be; the cheese a pale gooey mess and the bible paper thin slices of peperoni offering the hint of taste and spiciness, but not much more. But I still ate it. I did also have a side order of mac 'n' cheese, which was pleasant enough, but again could not quite live up to my expectations and hopes for it, like a son or daughter who gets not quite the degree you hoped they would.

Next morning, at breakfast, we were joined by Emma, and I was recounting the story of being stalked by a Mazda Bongo.

'That's my partner,' said Emma, 'and my son, they're following me to John O'Groats,' which explained a lot.

As we were leaving in the morning, I went over and spoke to Emma's partner, who was standing outside the van with two dogs.

'You're the guy who's stalking us,' I said.

He laughed. 'Not just you, all of you,' he said.

One of the dogs had three legs; it was missing one of its front legs. He also only had one ear but was a sweet looking animal, and I'm no great fan of dogs.

'I love the dog,' I said. 'How come it's only got 3 legs?'

'It's a rescue dog,' said the man, whose name was Mike. 'From Bosnia. When we got him, he had four legs; we took him to the vet, and he found hundreds of airgun pellets in his legs and ear, and they had to be removed.'

'He doesn't seem too bad with it,' I said, as the dog – its name was Nick – gambolled on the ground, waiting for his walk.

Mike and Ed, Emma's son who was 11, and the two dogs – Nick and a four-legged sausage one called Daisy – had started in Land's End and were making their way via a circuitous route, partly following Emma, to John O'Groats.

'How are you enjoying it?' I said to Ed, who had poked his head out of the door of the Mazda Bongo.

'It's great,' said Ed, 'I'm getting to see the country.'

'Enjoy,' I said to them all, 'see you on the road.'

I left them, the van packed with belongings, the man and the boy, the four-legged dog and the

three-legged, one eared dog, and Ian and I set off
into another sunny day, heading ever northwards.

Carlisle to Kilsyth

Miles: 112
Elevation: 6804ft
Ride time: 7h 39m
Average speed: 14.6 mph

*

## Saturday 27 August 2021

## Kilsyth, Scotland to Fort William, Scotland

We had gone about 10 miles, following a road beside the Caledonian canal, when I realised I had forgotten to hand in my key – either through simple forgetfulness, or some deep-seated unconscious Freudian revenge for having to wait for the key the night before. It was too late to go back, so I resolved to ask the Ride Leaders to let the hotel know that I would post it back when I got back home, which I did.

We soon reached the climb up Campsie Fell – a beautiful, almost alpine climb, with a few hairpins and some steepish sections but another quiet road without too many distractions. The sun had come up and it was another warm day, and the views from the climb were stupendous.

I pushed on ahead of Ian, as I did on all the climbs, slowing at the top for him to catch up, and then a glorious descent, possibly the second best descent I have ever done – second only to a descent in the Picos (the Puerto de San Glorio); some 3 miles or so, on a clear road, some pot-holes but with a clear view ahead so you could choose the best lines and lean into the bends, without worrying about some 10 wheeled motorhome looming suddenly out of the next bend.

And it was bright and clear, the sky cobalt and the sun shining, a faint breeze in the air; the sort of day and descent that cycling was designed for, the bike solid and comfortable beneath me, feathering the brakes as little as possible, and the first descent where Ian didn't catch me.

I waited at the bottom for Ian to catch up – we paused at the bottom as one of his cleats had worked loose, next to a sign for a farm called 'Bogside' which I thought was amusing, and then carried on to the town of Callander – a very busy town known as the gateway to the Trossachs. I tried to make an elaborate joke for Ian about a porn film called Callander Girls, but it was lost in the wind as we cycled and, in any case, probably wasn't funny enough to bear repeating here.

Callander was very busy and very hot, but we found a café – The Old Bank - with some tables and seats on the pavement outside, and settled down for some food, which was a long time coming.

I had a scone with butter and jam and a Lorne sausage roll, or Lorne sausage in a roll (to be precise), a delicacy of the area, although perhaps delicacy is giving it rather more weight than it can carry, which turned out to be square (the sausage, not the roll), but, apart from its shape, was much like any other sausage, in other words rather tasteless and in fact even more (less?) tasteless than most sausages. But it was food.

The thing about LeJog, as I may have already mentioned, is that apart from pedalling, the thing one thinks about most is food and quantity, regularity and calories is more important than what is eaten.

We left Callander and entered the Trossachs, along with about a million motorhomes, riding beside what looked like it might have been an attractive loch (Loch Lubnaig), but it was another busy road, and so I spent more time watching the traffic than I did admiring the scenery. Which was the case for much of the trip.

Heading up a long but not steep climb, on a busy two-lane road, assailed on both sides by the usual clutch of motorhomes and caravans, my eye was caught by a bridge or viaduct nestled in the hillside to our right, and looking uncannily like the one seen in all the Harry Potter movies. There was a lay-by there, perhaps put there for the benefit of passers-by who wanted a good view of the bridge, and a beautiful view down the hazy green valley, the loch shimmering in the distance.

Ian and I stopped and sat on the grass in the shade of a tree; I was glad of some respite from cycling as my arse was seriously aching – not saddle sores exactly, just the accumulated effect of sitting on a saddle for over 50 hours. I was using a Brooks Cambium C17 saddle with a cut-out which I had thought originally was quite comfortable, but perhaps any saddle would have struggled after that length of time. I had brought two of most items of kit on this trip but had only brought one saddle. I resolved that if there was to be a next time, I would bring a spare saddle, and ideally, a spare arse.

As we sat there in the relative silence of the view, about 15 massive motorcycles pulled in and all the riders – all of them aged about 70 - dismounted and started discussing the finer points of leather jackets and engine sizes.

'Let's go,' said Ian, who had had enough and was no more a fan of motorcycles than I was.

I was trying to think up original names for the lochs we passed, but after 'Padloch', 'Loch, Stock and Two Smoking Barrels' and 'Loch the door and throw away the key', I got bored and stopped. Further riding brought us to Tyndrum where we saw several not particularly appetising cafes, most of them patronised by motorcyclists, and instead stopped at the Tyndrum Inn for a rather leisurely lunch.

Ian and I both had soup, which was broccoli and very tasty it was, although I did find it repeating on me for the rest of the ride in a not very pleasant broccoli fumed way, and followed that with pasta, which once again turned out to be a bit of a disappointment. I had ordered chicken and pesto, but I could swear that it was chicken in tomato sauce, as it was reddish rather than greenish – perhaps chef opened the wrong packet. But pasta is still good calories while cycling, even if it's not very good pasta, if you know what I mean. And it came with garlic bread, which I did enjoy.

After Tyndrum we reached another long and busy climb, which – whether it was the soup or the pasta or the red chicken, or a combination of all three – I felt really motivated to attack and set off like a scalded cat, mostly in the big ring, storming up and passing many other riders on the way. We were now in the highlands.

'Where do the highlands start,' I asked Ian, after he caught up.

'After the lowlands,' he said, 'and after the medium lands, but before the not so quite highlands. Sterling, I always think.'

After the summit came the descent, across Rannoch Moor towards Glen Coe. This was a stunning but frankly scary and unsafe road and ride. It is a two-lane road, cut almost arrow straight through bleak moorland, with small lochs and swampy patches to either side, but there is no verge, so the road drops sharply down at the edges, meaning there is nowhere for a cyclist to ride, except in the road. And, with a steady stream of the now ubiquitous motorhomes as well as (probably) impotent men in expensive sports cars determined to exceed the speed limit and finding their way blocked by cyclists, a cyclist is constantly assaulted by beeping horns and cars swerving out to pass and then swerving sharply in again as they didn't realise a car might be coming the other way.

At one point near the iconic, much photographed and climbed (including by my mate Jon, he of the lift to Penzance) Buachaille Etive Mor, Ian and I were almost wiped out by a red Jaguar F-Pace which cut in sharply after overtaking and missed us by inches. Once across the moor, there was a long descent through the pass of Glen Coe (or Glenn Miller or Glen Hoddle as I insisted on calling it), where Ian swept past me, until we paused at the bright, shining, Loch Linnhe or Loch of my True Love's Hair as I preferred to call it, at the conclusion of the descent.

We then rode at the side of the loch all the way to Fort William. It was a well-surfaced road for the most part, with plenty of traffic, being one of the main routes up to the highlands, but wide enough that us cyclists were given a wide berth by most cars, although not of course Mercedes, Audis and Range Rovers, which for some reason and in every county of England and so far in Scotland, are cars almost invariably driven by knobs. Or cunts, as Ian and I called them.

Fort William did not strike me as a beautiful town by any means and indeed it wasn't, straggling along by the side of the loch, like long, lank, unkempt hair. Some of the group were staying at the Caledonia Hotel, which looked quite nice, but the rest of us were billeted in the Travelodge, right in the centre of town on the corner of the main street, with the usual bored receptionist sheltering behind a screen. My room was on the second floor, as it often seemed to be, the usual Travelodge box, but with most of the usual necessities including a bath, and a window overlooking the busy throughfare below.

I plugged in my electronics and checked Strava and was surprised and pleased to see that we had averaged 15mph for today's ride, and in fact seemed to be getting quicker as the week went on.

Outside I met Ian, Roy and Steve. The Travelodge did not have a restaurant, so we went looking for food.

'There's a Wetherspoons,' said Ian.

'I don't go in Wetherspoons,' I said, still harbouring a grudge over some (all) of Tim Martin's comments during the Brexit vote.

For some reason (thirst, possibly), Ian was determined to have a drink before dinner, but all the pubs and bars we visited had long queues.

'Saturday night on a Bank Holiday week-end in Scotland,' said Roy, 'what did you expect?'

The centre of Fort William was in party mood, but we were all hungry, and Ian was still thirsty. We finally found a bar that was open, although it said the restaurant was closed due to a shortage of staff.

The staff shortages on this trip were a common problem everywhere we went. From Penzance in Cornwall, where the hotel we stayed at had closed its dining room due to a lack of staff, to the numerous places that closed early or did not open at all, to the slow service in most of the cafes, the missing chefs and now this, staff shortages were felt through both countries. A combination of Brexit, Europeans going home and isolation due to Covid seemed to have made eating out a lucky (or unlucky) lottery.

We sat down in the bar and ordered drinks - gin and tonic for me.

'What sort of gin do you want?' said the barmaid, a question I was regularly asked but was unsure how to answer, as I thought Gordon's was the only gin in town.

'I don't care,' I said, 'the cheapest, or whatever the Queen Mother used to drink.'

'Gordon's then,' said the barmaid, who had perhaps met the Queen Mother.

Ian, Roy and Steve tucked into pints of beer and declared themselves happy.

As we sat drinking, Ian went on Google Maps looking for restaurants and phoned a few trying to book a table, but without success. We then noticed the bar-staff coming out with plates of food.

'I thought they didn't have any food,' I said.

Ian went to the bar to enquire.

'They do have food,' he said, when he returned, brandishing some menus as if they were trophies, 'it's just the restaurant that's closed.'

'Weird,' I said. But the menu looked decent enough, although with a slightly odd emphasis on Mexican, Cajun and Tex-Mex dishes.

'Must be the Alamo influence,' I said.

I had garlic bread with cheese on top, but again the cheese was barely cooked, and had the consistency (and taste) of melted latex gloves and followed that with Tex-Mex enchiladas; minced beef with tortilla chips, salad and salsa which was hot and spicy and tasty, although a bit short on carbs, as I found the next day.

I slept a bit better that night, although the Travelodge being on the main street and alcohol having flowed freely for a large portion of the night, I was not at all surprised to be woken at about 4am to the sound of shouting, drunken laughter, or laughter and drunken shouting, and perhaps all of it together. And furniture being thrown. What do people in the north have against furniture?

The Travelodge having no restaurant, our options for breakfast were limited, and we were advised by Martin to go to the Wetherspoons, which I was not happy about, but had little choice. Martin said the company would be paying for breakfast, which assuaged the irritation that many of us were feeling at some of the hotel choices on this trip.

The Wetherspoons did not open until 8am, and there was a quite a queue of bleary-eyed, still drunk people waiting outside, apart from us bright and bushy-tailed cyclists raring to go. It took a long time to get in, as everyone had to fill out a form before they could sit down, and the 'no mask, no entry' rule was strictly enforced.

There were 13 of our group eating here and Richard asked for it to all to be placed on one bill, so he could pay once.

'We cannae do that,' said the waiter, who had clearly been well trained by Tim Martin in customer service skills.

'I'm not paying 13 different bills,' said Richard, who was clearly in a belligerent mood, and who can blame him.

Eventually, the waiter relented, after making a call to Tim Martin, but he clearly wasn't happy about the situation.

I'd had enough of cooked breakfasts and instead ordered a sausage and egg muffin, a bacon and egg muffin and, in case I'd missed something, a sausage, bacon and egg muffin. They were not exactly inedible, but there was no butter on the muffins that I could discern, and they were also burnt, and the crisp, dry combination meant that they stuck to the roof of my mouth and were not easy to swallow, so I mostly just picked out the sausage, bacon and bits of egg and ate that instead. A mistake, as it turned out.

## Kilsyth to Fort William

Miles: 114
Elevation: 5945ft
Ride time: 7h 37m
Average speed: 15mph

*

## Sunday 28 August 2021

### Fort William, Scotland to Evanton, Scotland

Today was to be the shortest day of the whole trip, with a paltry 80 miles to cover. We soon left the unbeautiful Fort William behind on a quite cold, overcast day with a hint of dampness in the air and I was in front trying to catch a glimpse of Ben Nevis.

'Is that Ben Nevis?' I shouted to Ian, as we passed a foggy, mist-shrouded bump to our right.

'No,' he said, 'that's the Glen Nevis industrial estate.'

Whether it was my carb light dinner, or my carb light breakfast, or the days catching up with me, but I found today quite hard, and didn't have the energy in my legs I'd felt all week, and for the first time when we came to a climb, I let Ian go in front and had no inclination, or indeed ability, to go past him.

We reached Fort Augustus at the foot of Loch Ness and stopped at a pleasant café and gift shop, but it was very busy, with a curious serving system that gave the order to one person, who passed it to another, who passed it to another who couldn't then remember the order, like that game you play in management meetings about how easy it is for messages to get garbled down the line. I ordered coffee which eventually arrived, together with an egg mayonnaise sandwich and a scone with butter, jam and clotted cream. I wasn't sure if clotted cream was necessarily a good idea, but I was hungry and so forced it down, nonetheless. Mike, Emma's partner; Ed, her son and the two dogs were there when we arrived, having something to eat. I patted Nick, the three-legged dog.

'I like your dog,' I said to Ed.

'He's nice,' Ed said.

'I'll give you £50 for him,' I said.

'He's not for sale,' said Ed.

'Okay, £75 then.'

'No,' said Ed.

'You're a hard man to bargain with, Ed,' I said, 'I'll make it £100 plus a new iPhone.'

'I don't want an iPhone,' said Ed, 'I prefer Android.'

'Right, £500 plus an X-Box,' I said, 'take it or leave it.'

'No,' said Ed.

'He's a good kid,' I said to Emma.

'Enjoy the trip,' I said to Ed, 'I'll be asking questions at John O'Groats.'

I resolved to speak to my wife when I got home, about whether we could get a three-legged dog from Bosnia.

We ran into Mark and Charlie, or Sonny and Cher as I was now calling them. They had been billeted at the Caledonia Hotel in Fort William, which had seemed from the outside much nicer than the Travelodge.

'What was it like?' I asked.

'Awful,' said Sonny. 'Our room hadn't been made up. We got in and the beds hadn't been made, the bathroom was dirty and there was stuff on the floor.'

'Stuff?'

'Don't ask. I went downstairs to speak to the manager, and he said we'd done it! I said we'd only just arrived. Unbelievable.'

Mark and Charlie, being father and son, had decided to share a room, which was not a success. Mark, being older, snored and Charlie, poor fellow, got very little sleep all week, to add to the rest of his bad luck. He had struggled at the beginning of the trip with a sore knee, but as the days had passed, had got stronger and stronger and was now riding powerfully and purposefully towards John O'Groats.

'Go boys,' I said, as they rode off.

My wife Jane and I had married in 1990 and spent our honeymoon driving around Scotland. I remembered a strange bed and breakfast in Edinburgh, a very odd fanatically religious establishment on the Isle of Skye, a fascinating trip around Cawdor Castle, the waterfalls at Killiecrankie, a visit to the site of the Battle of Culloden, a night beside Loch Ness in Drumnadrochit visiting Castle Urquhart and trying and failing to catch any signs of the monster, and a blissful final 3 nights at Glenborrodale Castle on Ardnamurchan, which used up all of our money, so that we had to go home early. But it was worth it.

Drumnadrochit was our next stop on the ride and a restaurant for lunch. Another queue to get in, even though we were sitting outside (the Scots take test and trace very seriously, whereas in England no-one gives a shit), but a very friendly and helpful waitress. Ian and I were both hungry (again) so we both had courgette soup which was very tasty and then I ordered a Caesar salad, feeling desperate once again for some decent vegetables. Luckily, the soup came with bread and butter, so I still got my welcome carb ration.

Heading off from the restaurant, we rounded a few bends, and then a sharp right-hand hairpin which took us on to a horrible climb – initially quite benign, it then got steadily steeper and harder.

I was cold when we left Drumnadrochit and had put my wind jacket on, but half-way up this climb I was sweating like a bastard, so stopped and removed it. (That, of course, was the only reason I stopped). For only the second time on this trip – the first being the climb out of Wookey Hole – I was grateful for the 31/34 lowest gear on my Orbea bike. Ian, who came later, told me that there were ramps on the climb of 18 and 19% and I can well believe it. Once over the climb, the road was rolling, though quite bleak and empty territory with few cars and fewer people, a vast expanse of bleak Scottish territory all around, and us all alone, except for the other members of the group whom we passed, or were passed by, regularly.

There were more very long, very straight stretches of road, which were tiring to cycle on as the head wind, which we had been cursed with since the first day of the trip, necessitated constant pedalling with no break or respite.

We crossed a stone bridge and entered the Muir of Ord, a very romantic name for what proved to be a not very romantic place. There was a cycle lane beside the road on the bridge, but as usual it was full of debris and filth and other sharp objects designed to cause punctures, so I didn't ride in it.

'Get in the cycle lane,' shouted the passenger of an orange, shitkicker Mustang or similar American muscle car as it hurtled past over the bridge, delayed for precisely 3 seconds by this elderly cyclist on his trip of a lifetime. One gets so tired of drivers who do that – why do people in cars feel the need to shout at cyclists? And it's not just Scottish drivers, it happens everywhere – Kent, Cornwall, Cumbria, Devon, Wales: shit drivers, as Jesus memorably observed, are always with us.

Ian and I were both flagging a bit and found a café in the unpretty Muir of Ord – the Hub - that was still serving food, so we ordered coffees and all the cakes they had left – tiffin, mostly - and sat outside.

The route, which was following part of the North Coast 500 route, a famous route particularly for motorhomes, but also popular with cyclists (although I didn't think this part of it was very interesting – sorry) eventually took us to Evanton, and our hotel for the night, although some of the group were staying at a different hotel some miles further on. Ian I were grateful not to have to do those additional few miles.

This was another slightly odd hotel. There were obviously no other guests, although we did see some workmen at breakfast, so the Manageress said we could leave our bikes in the bar, which meant that all the available space was taken up with bikes. Going into the bar after getting changed, I ordered a gin and tonic.

'We don't have any spirits,' said the barmaid, although there were about 40 bottles of spirits lined up behind her. It was like a Monty Python sketch, or maybe those bottles were reserved for locals.

'Are they spirits?' I asked.

'We're not serving them,' said the barmaid, fiercely. Most of the guys ordered beer, but this proved a feat in itself, as you could have any beer you wanted, as long as it was Tenants, which was all they had, or at least all they were prepared to sell.

Whether due to shortage of staff, or for some other reason, we had had to pre-order our evening meal 2 nights before, when we were in Carlisle. However, of course no-one could remember what they ordered, so the poor waitress was bringing out plates of food and stood there while Martin called out names and the dishes that each person had ordered. I certainly couldn't remember what I had ordered until Marin reminded me. Mac 'n' cheese bites, which for some reason I thought was pasta but turned out to be something vaguely cheesy in a vaguely cheesy crumb with a meagre salad, and then a chicken penne dish which was very tasty and very spicy.

Harry, one of the riders, who needed his food gluten-free, found his pasta dish far too spicy and hardly ate anything, and instead went round the other diners trying to scrounge something gluten-free; without much success, I'm sorry to say, as no-one was prepared to share their food, everyone being hungry.

As we were finishing our meal, the Manageress came in and announced that the bar was closing at 8 o'clock; but people were welcome to buy something from the Co-Op down the road which stayed open until 10pm and bring it back and sit in the bar area. However, the only part of the bar area which had soft seats was shut and the other part of the lounge only had very uncomfortable hard-backed chairs and was surrounded by bikes, so was not the cosiest of environments, and so everyone basically just went to bed. Very strange.

Tomorrow is the last day!

The weather forecast is for colder temperatures with perhaps some rain, and Mike said it's still over 100 miles to go with 7000ft of climbing, so it's not over yet

Fort William to Evanton

Miles: 79.1
Elevation: 4177ft
Ride time: 5h 21m
Average speed: 14.8mph

\*

## Monday 29 August 2021

### Evanton, Scotland to John O'Groats, Scotland

The final day and then we've done it.

How am I feeling?

I'll be glad when it's over, to be honest. I've enjoyed the cycling; the cycling has not been too bad. Yesterday, the penultimate day, was hard, but the rest of the days – yes, they had their difficult moments, some tough climbs, some long boring stretches, and the head wind has been a pain every day, but overall, I didn't find it that hard. Although it hasn't finished yet – and the final day might break me! But I don't think it will.

However, the lack of adequate rest and recovery has been hard. One can train for consecutive long days on the bike (although I didn't), but it's hard to train your body and your mind to get used to the lack of proper rest and recovery. With so many restaurants closing early, we have had to get to dinner within about 30 minutes of arriving at the hotel, which has left very little time to do all those necessary things – putting electronics on to charge, checking Strava, washing clothes, undressing, showering, sorting out one's kit for the next day, etc.

I haven't slept well, although I don't normally sleep well, but not sleeping well when you're at home and not sleeping well when you're riding over 900 miles over 9 days are two completely different things. Last night I slept very little. I probably slept more than I thought I did, and some of that was dozing in that half sleeping, half awake mode, where you're asleep but dreaming you're awake, or awake but dreaming you're asleep. But either way, it doesn't give your body adequate rest and that is what you crave. There is a feeling of tiredness or, more accurately, fatigue which starts to overwhelm you as it builds up over the days. Maybe I'm just praying I get to the end, before the fatigue wins.

I had a couple of itches in the night – usual places, back of the knee, back of the elbow which I suppose must be midges, not that I've seen any. I did, however, make the mistake of having the window open for a short while when I got back yesterday.

But generally, all things considered, I feel…fine, actually; thanks for asking.

Have I enjoyed it?

Yes, it's been great – enjoyable, fun, challenging in places, stressful but not too stressful, and the close passes, the abuse, the crap roads (not always, but enough) were annoying, but no more so than when I'm cycling in Kent or anywhere else in this country.

The group has been fine: no-one has made a major nuisance of themselves or upset the group or tried to spread mad anti-vax theories, no-one has got Covid, there have been no accidents and, apart from the odd mechanical, Mark and Charlie's bad luck and my 3 punctures, it's been an incident free trip.

Ian and I have got on well – no fights, no arguments, no disagreements; we've ridden at a similar pace, not left the other behind or moaned about our riding styles. On a few occasions when I've been in front and raised myself off the saddle to ease my aching arse, Ian has shouted 'don't stop pedalling!' but I haven't let it get to me, and if he falls behind on the climbs, which he does, I'm happy to wait at the top for him.

We've ridden at our own pace and haven't tried to go with faster groups, although in fact there are few riders in this group who are faster than we are. Phil from Ballymena – a pilot, and the two Geordies that no-one can understand, they're quicker and stronger than we are, but then they're whippet thin and quicker than everybody, so we don't mind that. If I've learnt anything on this trip (and this is not new), it is the importance of pacing if doing long rides, or in this case a series of long rides. If you burn yourself out, either on one day or cumulatively, not only will you struggle to recover, but most of the enjoyment and all the fun will be gone.

Some of the hotels and rooms have been good, some less so – one doesn't need luxury, but one does want space, space to spread out, to fling one's kit on the bed, space to stretch, space to relax. For example, the room I had on this penultimate night, the bathroom was so tiny that the only way I could sit on the toilet was to shut the door and, even then, I had one foot in the shower, which is not conducive to relaxed bodily functions – the other thing that is so important on a trip like this.

Simply put, I would not do this trip if I had to share a room and luckily Ian feels the same way.

I was lying in bed last night; half awake and half asleep and I had a line of Leonard Cohen's which suddenly started going round and round in my head. I knew it was from the album 'Death of a Ladies Man', but I couldn't remember the actual song and I don't know why it suddenly came to me – it is not one of my favourite albums of his.

Anyway, it goes,

*It's like your visit to the moon*
*Or to that other star*
*I guess you go for nothing*
*If you really want to go that far.*

And I suppose that's a bit how I feel about LeJog. Land's End to John O'Groats is the longest distance between two points that you can do in Great Britain – obviously you could do a coastal trip around the coast which in total mileage would be longer - but in terms of going from A to B, this is the 'go to' iconic route, which I suppose is why it's the go to iconic route, and if you're a cyclist, it's what you do. So, there is a real sense of achievement in having done that – not, as I say, that I have done it yet!

If I think back to that video I made a couple of weeks before I set off: I said that, at the end of the day, I'm doing it because Ian asked me, and, as Mallory said of climbing Everest, because it's there.

Or, as Leonard Cohen sang, you go for nothing if you really want to go that far. And I did want to go that far – not before, I wasn't fussed, but now I'm so close, I <u>am</u> fussed, and I can't imagine not finishing it and not rushing down to that northern sea and grabbing a photo by the famous sign. You're doing it to do it and I'm doing it.

Paul Jones in his wonderful book, writes about how writing the book was his version of the end to end and he says everyone has their own end to end, even if it's not the actual end to end. And I've nearly done my end to end.

So, let's go and get this last day done and reach the end of the end to end.

It will be cold today and for the first and only time on this trip, I have donned leg warmers and a long-sleeved top, and dug out the neck warmer. The route today heads up the main A9, the coast road and for the most part it will be very exposed with the wind blowing in off the sea.

We left that strange hotel in Evanton, with its worrying resemblance to The Shining, at about 8.15.

Ian couldn't find his sunglasses which meant some serious faffing as bags were unloaded from the van and searched until they eventually turned up, but it meant that everyone else had already gone, including Emma who had slipped out at 6.30am to get a head start on everyone else.

The roads were quiet with very little traffic and after a few miles we hit our first climb, not hard but hard enough, and there was a damp mist hanging over everything, and about 5 minutes of rain, the only rain we encountered on this trip – the last downpour I had seen being a lifetime ago when Jon had driven me to Land's End and we had stood by the sign and watched the rain lash down on the lighthouse.

'Dreek' I believe is the Scottish word for this kind of weather. It looked like this would set in for the rest of the day, but in fact it didn't and although it remained resolutely colder than we had experienced so far, it stayed mercifully dry.

We caught most of the groups that had left before us, and crossed a very long, low, exposed bridge across the Dornoch Firth, before arriving at Golspie, where we saw the van and Martin directed us to the car park.

Ian was trying to enter a hairdressing salon before Martin pointed out that it was not in fact a café, and instead directed us to a café in the car park called the Coffee Bothy. All the cyclists in the group seemed to descend on it at very much the same time, and as they only allowed a couple of people in at a time, this meant very long queues. However, thanks to the furious pace I had set after crossing the bridge, Ian and I were among the first to arrive and were able to sit with our steaming coffees and groaning flapjacks while the others waited in the queue.

Two coffees and three cakes (one for Ian, two for me) came to £15.85 which struck me as fiendishly expensive. There was a public toilet in the car park which cost 50p to enter, which I thought extortionate – it was so expensive the machine accepted credit cards, but I did what everyone else did and waited until someone came out and then went in before the door shut. But it did strike me that with this grasp of economics, perhaps the Scots could make a success of independence after all.

Back on the bike, the landscape was not interesting and not what I expected. I had thought there would be a kind of austere, bleak beauty to it, a harsh land shaped by harsh winds and hardy people who bent this soil to their fierce will, but it just struck me as rather dull and flat and grey, and the small squat nondescript houses looked dreary and a bit sad and often in need of serious repair. This was not an area that exuded wealth.

We headed on up the plain coast, passing through a few small coastal villages, until we arrived in Helmsdale after about 50 miles and decided to have another break. We saw Mike, the (sort of) Ride Leader, now a paying customer, emerging from a side street and he directed us to a café which he said was worth a stop – called Thyme and Plaice; an odd name as, so far as I could tell, it sold neither herbs nor fish. However, the two owners, a husband-and-wife team, were exceedingly friendly and pleasant and Ian and I settled in for some proper food. Ian ordered soup as usual and a bacon sandwich while I had a cheese and pickle sandwich.

Ian engaged the woman in conversation as she had an English accent, and it transpired that she used to live in Beckenham in Kent, near me and used to work in the estate agents where my daughter rented her first flat. Such a small world! And she had moved from comfortable English suburbia to this small café, not exactly in the middle of nowhere, but certainly on the road to nowhere.

It was still cold, and I had put on my wind jacket over my long sleeved top and over that I put my Old Portlians gilet, which I had brought so that I could be photographed in my club kit, both at the beginning and end of the ride.

There was a long climb out of Helmsdale and then we continued to hug the coastline until we reached a long steep descent and then started the climb of Berriedale.

Berriedale is the other famous climb (after Shap Fell) from the end-to-end route, and Paul Jones describes the pain of the riders as they struggle up that last of the major inclines. It was about 10% for about half a mile or so, but I didn't find it hard – I might have had the best part of 900 miles in my legs, but I hadn't ridden it in under 2 days as the record holders had, so maybe that was the difference. But it was satisfying to know that the last of the famous hard climbs was over and nothing that came after would be as hard. Or so we hoped.

Mike had said in his final WhatsApp message that the landscape was spectacular, and I kept on expecting to round the next bend and have my jaw dropped with the stunning vistas and extraordinary scenery, but it never happened. It stayed dull and grey and rather nondescript and the bleakness, if it was there, eluded me.

The sea, off to the right-hand side, was also dull and grey, and if there were fearsome waves crashing on terrified rocks, we didn't see them. The heavy blanket of cloud didn't help either the landscape or my mood, determined, as I seemed to be, to find misery in every featureless feature of this dreary land.

There were more long stretches of flat, straight roads, with hard cycling into the wind until we reached Wick.

Wick was some 17 miles before the finish and both Ian and I needed a further energy boost for that final leg. The centre of Wick had seen better days, and even its better days had seen better days – boarded up shops, derelict buildings, even some of the pubs were shut and bolted. We did manage to find a warm and inviting café cum old time sweet shop called Morags and were just able to order a few snacks before they closed.

Morags had an old-style pick 'n' mix display, and I bought 100 grams of mixed chewy sweets, feeling the need for a sugar hit. Ian had soup (again) and I had some tiffin. The body does crave sugar on a ride like this – sugar in any form really; I had taken to grabbing the sachets of sugar from the tea and coffee making facilities in my hotel rooms and putting two sachets into each of my water bottles. And it seemed to help.

The last 17 miles to John O'Groats were across more flat and featureless lands – I had given up expecting things to change – past many derelict and tumble-down buildings, through the village of Keiss, a nasty little unexpectedly sharp little climb and then a long descent to our destination.

I had pushed on, head down, driving the pace and so was well ahead of Ian, so I paused at the John O'Groats village sign so that we could ride in together. We paused at the sign, took some photos, and shook hands awkwardly, before completing the final mile or so to the sea.

We passed the Sea View Hotel where we would stay our final night, Martin and the others who had finished already clapping as we sped past, and then the final few hundred yards, through a car park, jumped a kerb and then onto the small patch of land which contained the iconic sign. I didn't realise this ground was quite gravelly and lost momentum as soon as I reached it and almost fell off the bike but managed to remain upright. A couple stood by the sign, with their phone on a stick held in front of them for a selfie, and then Ian and I stood by the sign and took photos and had another awkward handshake.

We'd done it.

<u>Evanton to John O'Groats</u>

Miles: 102.7
Elevation: 5643
Ride time: 6h 59m
Average speed: 14.7mph

***

# Aftermath

We rode back to the hotel, where most of the rest of the group had already arrived and were busily packing away their bikes into their cardboard boxes.

It seemed strange to go into a hotel room and not worry about what kit to wear in the morning, or hurriedly fling some shorts and a jersey into the basin to soak or check Epic Ride Weather to find out how much wind there would be on our route in the morning.

For the only time on this trip, the room had two beds and that empty bed was eerie, as if my imaginary friend would turn out to be real and demand his (or her) bed for the night.

I changed and went down to the bar. Unlike the strange hotel in Evanton, this bar was not short of spirits.

'What gin do you want?' said the barmaid.

'What have you got?' I said.

'Up there, on the shelf,' she said, pointing to a cabinet above my head which ran the full length of the bar. There must have been 60 bottles.

'Gordon's is fine,' I said.

We sat in the bar in small groups, each with our own story to tell of that final day, the wind and the rain, the last few climbs, the final hurtle down to the sign, the elation and relief at finishing, that it was finally all over.

This was a larger hotel than some others and the dining room was full. We sat at tables of 6 due to Covid and the waiting staff brought out the food. As with the hotel in Evanton, we had had to pre-order this meal from a distinctly limited menu that the Ride Leaders had produced a few days ago, possibly in Carlisle, so long ago while we were still in England.

I had soup and then roast beef with potatoes and vegetables, good hearty English Sunday lunch fare, ideal preparation for a ride tomorrow, which we weren't doing. Mark and Charlie were both on our table and had ordered chips with their meal, but with no need to carb load, they had too many and sent them round the table for others to grab.

After the meal, Richard gave a little speech in which he congratulated everyone and said they were surprised that we had all made it – but I expect he said that to all the groups. And then we were given a certificate and a medal on a hideous Union Jack ribbon. We all put our medals around our necks and took photographs on our phones to post on social media. And then we went to bed.

I went to my room and laid on the bed, with the other empty bed looking accusingly at me, and recorded the final piece of this story on my voice recorder.

I thought back to the 7 reasons video that I had made, all those miles and climbs, potholes and bowls of soup back, and how many of those reasons were still valid.

I hadn't done it for charity, although some viewers to my YouTube channel had said they would donate some money to the food bank, if I finished. Pay up guys! And I did donate to the charities that Emma and Nick and some of the others were supporting. I have a strong suspicion that Kevan, who was riding for a charity for dogs, raised the most money, but that's dogs for you.

I couldn't tick it off my bucket list, because I didn't have a bucket list, but I could certainly tell people that I had done it and was joining that pantheon of LeJoggers, a select, if nonetheless quite large club.

Had I found myself? In a way, I had – I had found that I was, after all, quite a strong cyclist and could do this event, not easily that would be going too far, but relatively easy. Not easy then, but not hard, either. Eard? Heasy? I needed a new word – one that didn't sound like I was under-playing it but also didn't make it sound like one of Shackleton's journeys.

I'd enjoyed the challenge and pushed the envelope a bit – but the challenge of climbing the Mortirolo had been greater, and I had failed at the challenge of climbing the Angliru and I hadn't got my Raid Alpine medal because I packed on the climb of the Bonette, so there were still some real challenges left for me to do.

Alexander the Great wept when he was told there were no more worlds to conquer – I hope I never reach that position, so while there is still some strength in my legs, I can plan a crossing of the Alps in the company, or on the backs of, elephants. But I expect it's been done, with a 6-part documentary fronted by some minor celebrity already made, and a book written to tie in with the broadcast.

I'd escaped for 9 days from a life I wasn't desperate to escape from, but it gave my family a rest from hearing about cycling all the time.

I had discovered parts of Britain I wanted to see again: Dartmoor, the Somerset levels, the Clifton suspension bridge, the Wye Valley, the Scottish borders, the Lake District, Lancaster – the usual suspects, and some I didn't think I'd be rushing back to – Hereford, Warrington, Carlisle, although maybe we hadn't seen the best of those towns.

We left John O'Groats the next morning in a coach heading for Inverness and the sun was shining and the sky was blue, and the landscape looked very different and much less dull than it had appeared the day before, and I found a leaflet in the hotel about Caithness, showing the great number of Neolithic and Viking remains, so my view of that part of the Highlands changed, and I would like to return, perhaps in a campervan along with thousands of others.

But ultimately, as I said in my video, I did it because Ian asked me, and like poor Mallory had said, because it was there and it was a great adventure, and I'd loved every minute of it – even the punctures.

Roll on the next adventure!

\* \* \*

# Appendices

## Totals

The numbers for my ride are as follows:

Total miles ridden: 936.9
Total elevation: 56,818ft
Total ride time: 67h 28m
Average speed: 13.8mph
Total calories burned while riding: 37136[14]

## My bike

As I mention in the book, I had a choice of bikes to ride on this trip, including frames made of carbon, aluminium and steel, road or endurance set-ups and electronic and mechanical group sets.

I made a video before setting out, asking viewers to vote on whether I should take the Fairlight, the Mason or the Giant – I didn't have the Orbea at that stage. The result was as follows:

Fairlight Secan (steel): 51%
Giant Defy (carbon): 35%
Mason Definition (aluminium): 14%

The main reason people gave for their choice of the Fairlight was comfort – it offers a very comfortable

---

[14] This is the total number recorded on the Strava app. It is unlikely to be entirely accurate as it is calculated using the Strava algorithm, but it's accurate enough – whatever, it's a lot!

ride due to the combination of a steel frame, a relaxed geometry and large volume tyres.

I couldn't decide on which bike to take and seriously considered all three. I had ordered the Orbea – a carbon gravel bike – before deciding to go on this trip, and then decided I'd like to use it. My reasons were:

- It was a lightweight carbon frame and fork
- It had a more relaxed geometry – for comfort, particularly over long distances
- It had Shimano GRX gears – they are faultless in operation and the design of the brake hoods adds to the comfort
- It looks fabulous – never to be under-estimated!

The wheels it came with were quite heavy alloy wheels, shod with Vittoria Terreno Dry 38mm gravel tyres – more suitable for riding on gravel and relatively heavy. I therefore decided to use the wheels from the Giant – lightweight carbon wheels with 30mm tyres and I'm glad I did; the weight difference was significant – important on the hills.

<u>Details</u>

Orbea Terra - carbon frame and fork, size medium
Orbea handlebars, stem and seat-post
Shimano GRX810 mechanical group set
48/31 chain-set
11-34 cassette

Giant PSR One carbon wheels
Vittoria Corsa 2.0 30mm tyres
Brooks Cambium C17 saddle
Shimano mountain bike pedals

Cordel bar bag
Revelate top-tube bag
Speedsleev saddle bag

Silca pump
Exposure TraceR rear light
Lezyne front light

## Bike choice

Every rider in my group used a road bike with
dropped handlebars – no-one rode a flat bar or
mountain bike.

Some of them were fast road bikes with a more
aggressive geometry and some were endurance
bikes with a more relaxed geometry. Apart from
three riders on titanium bikes, all of the rest were
on carbon – no-one rode an aluminium bike.

The bikes ranged from a stonking Pinarello Dogma
F12 with electronic Dura-Ace Di2 gears, deep
section wheels and ceramic jockey wheels, which
couldn't have cost less than £12000; to an old
Merlin that John – he of the postcards – had
purchased for £400 from Gumtree after his own
bike was stolen.

In selecting a bike to ride for LeJog, my advice would be that you should ride whatever bike you own that you feel most comfortable riding. With over 900 miles to cover and about 8 hours in the saddle most days, comfort is more important than out and out speed. If you're lucky enough to have a choice of bikes or are thinking of buying a new bike for the trip, then I would suggest choosing one with a more relaxed, often called 'endurance' geometry. Gravel bikes are very popular currently and they make a good choice, although I would suggest changing the tyres – they often come with tyres of 40mm width or greater – perhaps to 32mm or 30mm.

I would not recommend getting a new bike less than 3 months before embarking on the trip, as you need time to get used to it, be comfortable on it, as well as identifying any little issues that might need correcting. In other words, don't do what I did and use a bike that was 2 weeks old! In my defence, I had hoped to get the bike sooner, but it was delayed by Brexit and Covid.

Whichever bike you decide to ride, it is vital that you have a complete service done before you start. By 'complete' service, I mean one where the bike is stripped down and all components are fully checked and replaced where necessary. I suggest you tell the bike shop that you are doing LeJog, so that they fully understand the importance and reason for the service. Consumable items, such as brake blocks, discs, cables and chains are relatively inexpensive, and if they show any signs of wear, I recommend that you have them replaced.

When Nick had his accident on the climb up to Ludlow, he bent the hanger for his rear derailleur. The hanger is designed to fail if the bike falls over like this, as it is cheaper to replace the hanger than it is to replace the rear derailleur. If the hanger gets bent, it is possible to bend it back again, but it has been weakened and is therefore liable to break; this was the reason for Martin's advice to Nick not to ride the bike. The mechanic at the bike shop that Nick went to - Rock Garden Cycles – was clearly very careful and skilful and was able to straighten the hanger without breaking it.

Rear mech hangers come in many different sizes and are not standardised – it is therefore not surprising that the Bike Adventures support van did not carry a spare. I strongly advise that if undertaking any long bike trip, you buy a spare mech hanger for your bike and carry it with you, for just this type of situation where the bike falls over and lands on the drive-train – it is by no means uncommon, and a mech hanger weighs very little.

One of the advantages of using the Fairlight, had I done so, is that the mech hanger is also made of steel and is part of the bike, and can therefore be bent back.

Saddles are a personal choice and I'm not sure that any saddle feels perfect after 60 hours siting on it!

However, resist the temptation to buy a new saddle on a friend's or magazine recommendation one week before the trip – you need a saddle which you are used to, and your bottom is familiar with!

I used a Brooks Cambium C17 saddle with a central cut-out which I was mostly happy with, although my rear suffered in the latter days.

## Tyres, tyre boots, tubes and tubeless

I also made a video about tyre choices before embarking on the trip. I considered various brands – Continental, Pirelli, Vittoria, Hutchinson - and various tyre widths – 28mm, 30mm, 32mm, 35mm and 38mm. Eventually I settled on the Vittoria Corsa 2.0 30mm tyres. Although not new, I had been riding them on the Giant and had probably covered less than 600 miles on them. They were comfortable, fast rolling, I had not had any punctures in them and with tan walls they looked the business!

As it transpired of course, I had 3 punctures in the first 3 days, although nothing thereafter.

I had considered purchasing some new tyres for the trip and was looking for some Continental GP5000 30 or 32mm tyres, but due to a combination of Brexit, Covid and world-wide shortages of bikes and bike equipment, was unable to find any.

When I found the puncture in my hotel room in Wookey Hole, I removed a tiny piece of glass from the tyre, which left a tiny hole. Concerned about getting a fourth puncture, I covered the hole with a piece of tyre boot. A tyre boot can be purchased from any bike shop and is a small square or rectangle of some plasticky material which can be stuck to the inside of the tyre to cover a hole; I recommend you carry one in your saddlebag. If you don't have a tyre boot, you can use a 5, 10, 20 or even £50 note, or do as one of my friends did - cut a piece from a toothpaste tube and carry that with you – it also works.

You may be lucky on your trip and not get any punctures – and indeed most of the riders on our trip did not have any – but it is best to be prepared. I have learnt, from bitter experience, that it is best to carry two tubes on a long ride and this I did; some people I know carry three. Being a supported ride, the van had spare tubes for sale, and I ended up purchasing two, as well as one I purchased from the bike shop in Crediton.

The Tubolito tubes I used are a relatively new product. They are made of thermoplastic, as opposed to butyl or latex, are smaller and lighter than normal tubes and are supposed to be more puncture resistant. Whether due to bad luck, enemy action or act of God, they did not work for me, but who knows – they may work perfectly for you.
In a similar vein, my experience of tubeless tyres has not been a happy one. I have tried different tyres on many different rides, but I always seem to have some problem or other and I have now given up on tubeless. However, they are becoming more

and more common, and plenty of riders swear by them, including riders in our group, so if they work for you - use them.

However, as with all kit, my advice is not to go tubeless a few weeks before your trip; you need to spend some time getting used to them and learning how to deal with any issues which may arise.

## Pedals, cleats and shoes

The majority of riders in my group were using road pedals – Look or Shimano - with road cleats and shoes. If you are unfamiliar with these, they are the sort of shoes that Tour de France and other professional cyclists use – the cleats sit proud of the sole of the shoe which makes them difficult to walk on, certainly for any length of time.

If you are a dyed-in-the-wool 'roadie' who would not be seen dead in anything other than road shoes, then wear them! However, if you are not, or are thinking of using cleats for the first time, or you are deciding what is best to use for a trip like this, my strong advice is to use what are commonly referred to as mountain bike pedals, cleats and shoes.

With these, the cleat is recessed into the sole of the shoe making them much easier and more comfortable to walk in. They are also less likely to damage wooden or other floors, which saves you having to remove your shoes when you enter a hotel, restaurant or pub. You can buy rubber cleat covers to put over the cleats, but it is one more thing (or two) to carry and I invariably forgot to put them on when I wore road shoes.

You may recall early in my book that on the first day David took his shoes out of the bag and one of the boa dials was broken. Boa dials – you turn a small dial which tightens a plastic wire which fastens the shoe – are very common, particularly on road shoes and they offer a very fine level of adjustment. However, in rare cases they can become loose or worn. Partly for this reason, I wore a pair of Quoc shoes, which used laces; laces or Velcro straps are less likely to go wrong.

If you do use road shoes with road cleats, I strongly suggest carrying a spare pair of shoes and, if not, I would carry spare cleats. You may recall from the book that Charlie broke one of his cleats – road cleats, because they are in contact with the ground when walking, can wear very quickly, particularly if you are walking on gravel or other rough surfaces.

## Training and fitness

I am not an expert on training and there are many books available on the subject, as well as a wealth of information on the internet, including training plans for you to follow as you prepare for this sort of trip – so what follows is from my own personal experience; you may nonetheless find it useful.

As I say in the book, I did not find riding LeJog difficult, which is not to say that it was easy – it wasn't. However, I do believe that most cyclists could undertake this trip, but they would certainly benefit from some specific training.

It may sound obvious and trite but there is no better way to prepare for a long multi-day ride than to ride your bike. The more miles you can get into your legs the better, so if you have been riding regularly for several years you are half-way there. (I have been riding regularly for about 10 years and normally ride about 5-7000 miles a year). Try and prepare for this trip some months in advance – the earlier the better.

If you are working and it is possible for you to commute to work by bicycle, then do so. If you can't, then try to cycle during the week and not just at weekends. If that means getting up early and doing an hour before work, or an hour when you get home, then do so. If the weather is bad and you don't want to ride (but do remember you may have bad weather on your LeJog, so you'll have to do it sometime!), then get a turbo and ride indoors. Zwift, Trainer Road and Sufferfest are excellent programmes to use, and they all offer a variety of training programmes.

You will be doing long rides on LeJog – up to and often over 100 miles – so it is important that you undertake several long rides during your preparation. You will also be doing long rides day after day, so it is essential that you undertake some multi-day (2 or 3 or 4 days) rides, back-to-back. Riding 100 miles in a day is one thing, doing 100 miles day after day is quite another, and you need to get used to how it feels.

I had a plan to do several 200-mile weeks, followed by 300-mile, 400 mile and even a 500-mile week during my preparation. In the end, for various reasons, I didn't but it was and is still a good plan.

You will be doing a lot of climbing on the LeJog route, so hill repeats and practice will also be beneficial. There is no need to try and ride up hills quickly, but you need to get used to doing it. On LeJog you will do some short, steep climbs, some long, steep climbs and some long but not very steep climbs. Try and find an example of each on your ride and practice on them.

It is also a good idea to do intervals – short periods of high intensity riding followed by rest, repeated several times. This can be done on the road but is ideal for doing on the turbo or in the gym and have the advantage that they can be done in a short space of time.

It is also a good idea to perform exercises off the bike. Squats are very good for strengthening the legs and any exercise which strengthens your core is also beneficial. Some riders experience back pain or other pain while riding – I recommend a bike fit to check whether there are changes to your set-up that might help – although I would advise not doing this less than about 3 months before your trip – you need time for your body to get used to any changes.

A bike fit might also suggest changes if you are prone to neck pain when riding long distances, but if you are able to ride a bike with a more relaxed, endurance focussed geometry, this will be better, as you will have a more upright position, rather than an out and out road bike which is likely to put you in a position where you are lower over the handlebars.

It is not easy to train for the lack of adequate rest which you will experience, but a few simple measures on the trip can assist in getting a good night's sleep. Avoid eating late at night if you can and avoid looking at your phone or iPad screen immediately before going to sleep. A hot bath or shower before going to bed can also help.

To assist your body to recover after each long ride, it is a good idea to learn some of the key stretches for cyclists – there are many resources and videos on the internet – and to do these both before and after each ride. Many cyclists swear by yoga and feel it is beneficial to them.

I brought a roller for my muscles and used it a few times; I should have used it more often, and some of the members of the group had one of those new-fangled massage guns and expressed themselves satisfied with what it did for them.

The best advice I can give for doing the ride itself is to ride at your own pace, particularly on the hills. Try and resist the temptation to ride with people who are faster and stronger than you – do this in your training (it will pay dividends) but don't do it on LeJog. If you are going with a friend with similar ability to you, ride with them; if not, and you are joining an organised group as I did, you will almost certainly find someone with similar abilities to you; ride with them.

## Nutrition

I am not by any means an expert on nutrition and do not really understand the whole sugar/glucose/calories/energy/carbohydrate/protein stuff – to put it scientifically - so I shall confine my advice to a few key points.

First, fluid intake is tremendously important – you must keep drinking! This is quite easy on a hot day as you feel thirsty but is less easy on a cold day as you will feel less like drinking. However, you must do, as dehydration can have a significant impact on your performance. Most people will put electrolyte tablets in their bottles – you will have your own preferred brand; personally, I like the taste of High 5 – but I also added 2 sachets of sugar which I took from my hotel room.

Second, you should eat 'proper' food, especially at lunchtime; don't try and get by on energy bars, gels, cakes and sweets all the time – useful sources of energy though they may be. Some riders love gels, while others can't stand them; if you do use them, try not to have too many during a ride as they can play havoc with your digestion. Good alternatives to gels are nuts, dates, figs, dried apricots, bananas (every cyclist's favourite), and raisins.

I craved pasta on this trip, but it wasn't much in evidence; good alternatives are jacket potatoes, rice, sandwiches – ideally brown or wholemeal bread, rather than sliced white – soup (Ian's favourite) pork pies or pies in general and baked beans. It is best to avoid too much fatty food, such as sausage rolls or bacon sandwiches, much as you might enjoy them, as they can be hard to digest when you get back on your bike.

I also recommend that you eat a hearty breakfast – porridge, muesli or cereals are a good choice – and a good, solid evening meal with plenty of carbohydrate – rice, pasta, potatoes, etc. On a few evenings I had a pudding and sometimes carrot cake at a café stop which always went down well, but I advise against eating too much cream.

I lost weight before going on the trip – deliberately – but don't believe I lost any weight on the trip itself, which I think is a good thing, as it meant that I was consuming sufficient calories.

## Kit list

This is a list of everything I took on the trip. As it was a supported trip and the luggage was being transported, obviously I was able to take more than I could have done if it was a self-supported trip.

*Cycling kit*

3 short-sleeved jerseys
2 long-sleeved jerseys
1 gilet
3 pairs of bib shorts
3 short sleeved base layers
1 long sleeved base layer
1 wind-proof long sleeved base layer
1 rain cape
1 packable rain/wind jacket
1 pair of mitts
1 pair of full finger cold weather gloves
Leg warmers
Knee warmers
Arm warmers
Neck warmer
Neckerchief
2 caps
Shoe covers
Cycling shoes
5 pairs of socks
Warm jacket
Helmet

*Casual clothes*

2 long-sleeved shirts
1 polo shirt
1 T-shirt
2 pairs of trousers
Fleece jacket
Thin jacket
Shoes

Underwear

*Electronics*

GoPro Hero 7 black – action camera
Canon G7X Mk ll – compact camera
2 power banks
USB charging adapter with 5 ports
4 USB micro cables
2 USB-C cables
iPhone and Apple watch cable
Spare batteries
Spare SD cards
Amazon Fire tablet
Olympus LS-P4 voice recorder
Earphones

*Toiletries*

Toothbrush
Toothpaste
Razor
Shaving oil
Deodorant
Shampoo
Travel wash
Nurofen
Hay fever tablets
Sun lotion
Chamois cream
Assos skin repair cream
Band-aids
Sterilising tablets

*Other*

Muscle roller
Spare cleats
Ass saver
Wahoo Elemnt Bolt and Roam
Chain lubricant
Heart rate strap
ID bracelet
2 pairs of prescription cycling glasses
Energy bars - Veloforte
Energy gels – Veloforte and Kendal
Electrolyte tablets – High 5
Insect repellent

## Camera choice

Many riders will want to do as I did and make a video of their end-to-end experience, and if not make a video at least take lots of photos. Most riders in my group used their phones to take photos, and the cameras in modern phones are superb.

I used two cameras for shooting video: a GoPro Hero 7 Black for on-bike footage and a Canon G7X Mk ll for most other filming.

I put the GoPro in a Revelate top tube bag, which opens with a flap secured with a magnetic clasp, making it easy to open the bag and remove the camera with one hand – important while cycling! The GoPro was on a mouth mount, which I could either hold in my hand, or put in my mouth, meaning I could keep both hands on the handlebars. The GoPro was in a foam housing to reduce wind noise through the microphone.

The Canon was in a front handlebar bag, and I generally used this when we stopped. I also used it in my hotel room at night or in the early morning – set up on a small tabletop tripod - to record pieces to camera.

I planned to write an account of the trip – this is it! – but knew it was unlikely that I would feel like sitting down in the evening to write out any notes; as it transpired I didn't, but in any case, I also had very little time. I therefore brought along an Olympus LS-P4 voice recorder and recorded an account of the day's events shortly before I went to bed, and this worked very well.

## Supported or unsupported

I may not be too old to go camping, but I am too old to *want to* go camping, so a self-supported camping trip was never going to be on the cards. I could have done what some friends did and gone unsupported but sent baggage to the next stop each morning by taxi. But it seemed like a faff to me.

I'm at an age when I like my creature comforts – even if in an Ibis Hotel they are in short supply – so preferred the relative ease of a supported trip, where Bike Adventures booked the accommodation, planned the route, transported the luggage, and provided some support during the day.

But if you're an experienced long distance multi-day cyclist, used to carrying all your kit with you, then you will already know what you prefer to do.

With the luggage transported by van, I was able to carry sufficient kit, and in fact ended up bringing several items that I didn't need – although that was partly due to the weather; I did not need most of the rain and cold weather kit which I had brought.

Obviously, if you are carrying everything on the bike, you will have to be much more ruthless in leaving things behind, when weight will be at a premium. Bike-packing, or more lightweight touring is very popular now, but a nine-day (or longer) trip is almost certainly going to require a pannier set-up, unless you want to travel very light.

The other consideration of course, is cost – my Bike Adventures trip cost £1450 plus the single room supplement of about £300. This covered accommodation, breakfast and luggage transport, but not lunches and not the evening meal (except the final evening meal in John O'Groats), and not travel to Penzance (I was lucky to get a lift from Jon), or travel back from John O'Groats, except as far as Inverness. I did not look at other companies – there are many that offer the end-to-end trip – but I doubt if the price would be substantially different. Apart from food and drink, I did not buy anything while I was away; not even a postcard – unlike John.

## Other tips and suggestions

*Sugar in your bottle*

Sugar, as any fule kno, is the key energy source while on the bike. I carried 2 water bottles each containing water and 2 High 5 electrolyte tablets.

However, I also took to taking the sachets of sugar which were placed in my hotel rooms with the tea and coffee making facilities and adding two sachets to each bottle. When we stopped at a café or for lunch, I added another sachet or two to the bottle when I re-filled it.

The extra sweetness tasted nice and added an additional energy boost while I was riding along.

*Power bank*

As you will almost certainly be using some form of bike computer, or your phone, you will risk exhausting the battery life before you have competed a long ride. It is a good idea to carry a small power bank and either charge your device as you ride along or put it on charge when you stop for lunch. However, ensure that you carry the correct cable connection!

## Sunscreen

Riding outside for 8 hours or so each day will lead
to sunburn, even if it is a cloudy day, so always
apply sunscreen before you set off. Being a former
red head (it is mostly grey or white now), means
that I have pale skin and need to be careful in the
sun. It is probably a good idea to re-apply
sunscreen when you stop for lunch.

## Drying your kit

Riding for nine days will inevitably require the
washing of clothes, unless you want to carry nine
pairs of shorts! Do not be tempted to wear the same
pair of shorts for more than one day without
washing them – you will risk saddle sores which
could end your trip prematurely.

Carry a small bottle of travel wash and wash your
kit as soon as you get to your hotel room. I found it
best to wash something every day, otherwise you
risk having to do a big load when you least feel like
it.

Having washed your kit, wring it out and then
hang it up in the bathroom for an hour or so – more
moisture will have collected which you can then
wring out.

Next, take a hand towel from the bathroom and lay
it on a flat surface, such as your bed. Place the kit
on the towel and then roll it up like a Swiss roll.
Wring it out hard several times, hang it up and you

should find that your kit is dry in the morning. If there is a heated towel rail, use that but do not be tempted to put your kit on a fan heater – you will risk starting a fire.

If you should find that your kit is still damp in the morning – mine always dried satisfactorily – use the hairdryer which you will have in your hotel room.

*Getting home from the end*

Your travel choice to get home from John O'Groats will depend on your circumstances and where you live.

Bike Adventures had laid on a coach which dropped some people off at Inverness station – about 2 hours' drive from John O'Groats – and some at Inverness airport. Most of the bikes – packed into the cardboard boxes – were sent on separately by courier.

Ian and I had arranged a hire car to be collected from Inverness airport. We then drove to Shropshire where Ian lived to drop him off; a journey of some 8 hours, including stops. I stayed the night and then drove to Kent where I live to drop off my kit, before driving to Gatwick Airport to drop off the car.

This worked well, but make sure the car you hire is big enough to take your bike(s) and luggage.

Whenever and however you decide to ride LeJog, I wish you the best of luck – and above all, enjoy the experience!

**The End
of the
End-to-End**

West Wickham, Kent - September 2021

Old Friends to
the End

073687

Printed in Great Britain
by Amazon